HOW TO

JUMP HIGHER

HOW TO
JUMP HIGHER

**James A. Peterson
and
Mary Beth Horodyski**

mp
MASTERS PRESS

A Division of Howard W. Sams & Company

Published by Masters Press (A Division of Howard W. Sams & Co., A Bell Atlantic Co.)
2647 Waterfront Pkwy. E. Dr., Suite 300
Indianapolis, IN 46214

10   9   8   7   6   5   4   3

Library of Congress Cataloging-in-Publication Data

Peterson, James A. 1943 —
        How to jump higher / James A. Peterson and Mary Beth Horodyski.
            p.   cm.
        Bibliography: p.
        ISBN 0-940279-12-6
        1. Jumping — Training.   I. Horodyski, Mary Beth.   II. Title.
GV1073.P47   88-836
796.4'32'07 — dc19   CIP

To the Corps of Cadets, past, present and future:

The best of America's young adults, becoming better through hard work and an unwavering commitment to excellence.

TABLE OF CONTENTS

PREFACE ix

PART ONE: UNDERSTANDING HOW YOU JUMP

CHAPTER 1: VERTICAL JUMP BASICS

      The Role of the Vertical Jump in Athletics 3

      Assessment Procedures 4

      Vertical Jump Score Norms 5

      Programs to Increase Vertical Jumping Ability 5

CHAPTER 2: THE MECHANICS OF JUMPING

      The Nervous System and Movement 7

      The Muscles Involved in Vertical Jumping 14

      The Next Step 14

PART TWO: IMPROVING YOUR VERTICAL JUMP

CHAPTER 3: STRENGTH TRAINING

      Basic Fundamentals and Techniques 20

      What Equipment Should You Use? 21

      What Guidelines Should You Follow? 22

      What Program Should You Adopt? 24

      Training Exercises

      Free Weights 30

      Universal Gym 53

      Nautilus 66

      Partner Resistance Exercises 82

CHAPTER 4: PLYOMETRIC TRAINING

      Fundamental Guidelines and Techniques 102

      Plyometric Drills 104

CHAPTER 5: MENTAL TRAINING

      Seven Mental Skills for Improving Your Vertical Jump 116

APPENDIX A: THE BACKMATE® WORKOUT PROGRAM 121

APPENDIX B: THE ULTRA-ROPE® TRAINING SYSTEM 125

REFERENCES 129

PREFACE

The effort to develop *How to Jump Higher* as a book grew out of our concern that in their haste to develop this critical motor skill, athletes were expending an extraordinary amount of energy and resources on programs and activities that, at best, are a waste of time and, at worst, subject the athlete to the unnecessary likelihood of being injured. *How to Jump Higher* presents a comprehensive overview of how athletes can effectively increase vertical jumping ability. We attempted to write it for athletes, men and women alike, at all competitive levels of sports. If you follow the programs and guidelines presented in *How to Jump Higher,* you will develop your vertical jumping ability to the best of your God-given potential.

Keep in mind that, our best wishes to the contrary, not everyone has the potential to be a Michael Jordan or a world-class volleyball player. All you can do is make the best of your genetic capabilities. This book will enable you to accomplish that goal. Good luck and good jumping.

James A. Peterson, Ph. D.

Mary Beth Horodyski, A.T.C.

PART ONE

UNDERSTANDING HOW YOU JUMP

1

VERTICAL JUMP BASICS

THE ROLE OF THE VERTICAL JUMP IN ATHLETICS

Vertical jumping ability often plays a critical role in sports performance. Your ability to jump higher than your opponent can, all other factors being equal, enable you to achieve a much higher level of success in the athletic arena. As a component of specific sports skills, vertical jumping ability is a vital motor skill that can be improved to a limited degree. Sports skills that involve vertical jumping include rebounding and shot blocking in basketball, spiking and blocking in volleyball, high jumping and long jumping in track and field, pass receiving and pass defense in football, heading the ball in soccer and controlling the lineouts in rugby. Anyone with a good working knowledge of athletics could produce a much more exhaustive and comprehensive listing of these skills.

Since an athlete's ability to jump higher frequently has a major impact on the outcome of the contest in which the athlete is competing, it is hardly surprising that coaches and athletes are often preoccupied with improving this important motor ability. The extent of this preoccupation varies from individual to individual and from sport to sport. It would not be an exaggeration, however, to conclude that, at a minimum, most coaches focus their efforts involving vertical jumping ability on two areas: evaluation (measurement, comparison, and retesting) and development (identifying and implementing a program for increasing an athlete's ability to jump higher).

ASSESSMENT PROCEDURES

The procedure for empirically measuring how high an individual can jump has been fairly standardized over the years.* Figures 1.1 and 1.2 illustrate the steps commonly used to measure vertical jumping ability. First, the athlete stands sideways next to a wall on which the height has been marked in one-inch or two-inch increments above a certain point. The athlete is instructed to put chalk on the fingertips of his or her dominant hand and extend the hand as high as possible and touch the wall (Figure 1.1).

Figure 1.1   Figure 1.2

---

* The procedures described in this section are typical of those followed in most organized athletic programs. Individuals involved in pure research endeavors often use more precise steps and equipment to assess vertical jumping ability — an approach that simply is too impractical for most coaches.

The height the athlete can reach while standing is then recorded. Next, the athlete is directed to jump as high as possible and again touch the wall. The athlete's vertical jumping score is obtained by subtracting the reach-height mark, while standing, from the maximum height achieved during the vertical jump. Usually, the individual being tested is not permitted to take a preliminary step before jumping. Most testing assessment involves multiple — usually three to five — attempts for each athlete.

VERTICAL JUMP SCORE NORMS

A limited number of studies that have been made attempting to identify vertical jumping score norms for selected groups. Young men — as a result of physiological differences between themselves and young women — jump higher than their female counterparts. Age also affects how high an individual is able to jump. To a point as a person get older, vertical jumping ability improves as the muscular system develops.

As a coach or an athlete, you should keep in mind that the vertical jumping norms you might use for comparative purposes are averages. As such, they are subject to a myriad of limitations regarding their usefulness and application for you or your program. Certainly, the NBA general managers who passed on Larry Bird in the 1980 NBA draft because of their preconceived notions of his alleged "lack" of jumping ability have had the opportunity to reconsider their positions in the last several years.

PROGRAMS TO INCREASE VERTICAL JUMPING ABILITY

The other area in which coaches focus their efforts concerning vertical jumping ability involves identifying and implementing steps to improve their athletes' jumping ability. Some coaches adopt programs that purport to improve vertical jumping ability in an efficient, effective manner, but which unfortunately do not. These programs are not based on sound principles, but instead often involve gimmicks, intuitive guesswork and a wide variety of "no-pain, no-gain, you-can't-do-too-much" prescriptions.

Any approach that does not adhere to sound scientific principles is, at best, counterproductive. This book was written on the basic premise that each person deserves to make the best of his or her God-given abilities. Chapter 2 presents an overview of the role your nervous system plays in performing a motor skill (vertical jumping) and a listing of the musculature involved in jumping. The last three chapters examine the three most effective developmental methods for improving your ability to jump higher: strength training, plyometric training and mental training. Combined with specificity training*

---

* Specificity training essentially means that the single best method for improving a specific task is to practice that task. In other words, if you want to jump higher, your developmental program must actually include practicing jumping.

(actually practicing vertical jumping), these training regimens give you a sound, scientific basis for being able to jump higher.   Making a commitment to improving yourself is a significant initial step. Translating that commitment into positive results will require a lot of work on your part. The information in this text is designed to insure that your efforts are not wasted.

CHAPTER 2

THE MECHANICS OF JUMPING

The two primary systems of the body that are involved in jumping are the nervous system and the muscular system. The body employs certain mechanisms to receive and translate sensory input to initiate movement, but the location where movement is initiated is unknown. The muscles that are innervated are the agents through which movement is actually achieved.

The neuromuscular involvement of a motor skill, such as vertical jumping, is very complex. In order to better understand the mechanics of jumping, this chapter presents a basic overview of the way in which your nervous system initiates movement and an inclusive listing of the muscles that are involved in vertical jumping.

THE NERVOUS SYSTEM AND MOVEMENT

Several areas of your nervous system are involved whenever you perform a motor skill. Motor learning experts suggest that the primary part of the brain involved in movement is the cerebral cortex, which is where thought processes begin. The basic areas of the nervous system that are involved in performing a motor skill are listed and defined in Table 2.1. The cerebral cortex contains the sensorimotor area, which is located just anterior (motor functions) and posterior (sensory functions) to the central sulcus. Stimulation of the sensorimotor area will elicit muscular contraction.

Table 2.1 Definitions of Selected Aspects of the Neuromuscular System

BASAL GANGLIA: Masses of grey matter in the cerebral hemisphere that play a major role in motor activity and are closely related to the brain stem centers.

BRAIN STEM: The portion of the brain remaining after the cerebral hemispheres and cerebellum have been removed. Collected in this complex extension of the spinal cord are numerous neuronal circuits, some of which are involved in movement.

CEREBELLUM: The part of the brain that lies below the cerebrum and above the pons and the medulla oblongata. It is involved with coordination of muscular action and with bodily equilibrium. It monitors and makes corrective adjustments in the motor activities elicited by other parts of the brain.

CEREBRAL CORTEX: The cortex of the cerebrum—the largest part of the brain. Consisting of two equal-sized hemispheres, the cerebrum is believed to control conscious and voluntary processes.

CORTICOCEREBELLAR TRACT: One of the basic afferent (transmitting toward) pathways of the cerebellum.

CORTICOSPINAL TRACT: Also referred to as the pyramidal tract. This is one of the major pathways by which motor signals are transmitted from the motor areas of the cerebral cortex to the spinal cord.

GOLGI TENDON ORGANS: Small receptor organs that are within muscle tendons immediately beyond their attachments to muscle fibers. Their major responsibility is to detect the amount of tension in the muscle and to transmit signals to the spinal cord to cause reflex effects in the involved muscle.

INTERNEURONS: Small, highly excitable neural cells that are found in all areas of the grey matter in the spinal cord. Capable of firing as rapidly as 1,500 times per second, they directly innervate the anterior motorneurons which, in turn, give rise to the nerve fibers that leave the spinal cord and proceed to the muscle fibers.

JOINT RECEPTORS: Sensory receptors found in and around skeletal joints that signal the exact position of the joint to higher neural centers. It is thought that the various patterns of the signals resulting from each of the possible positions of a joint influence bodily movement by affecting the motorneurons of the muscles.

MEDULLA OBLONGATA: The widening continuation of the spinal cord forming the lowest part of the brain and containing vital nerve centers for the control of such critical functions as breathing and circulation.

MOTORNEURONS: Nerve cells that conduct movement impulses which innervate muscles. Together with its associated muscle cells (fibers), a motorneuron is the integral foundation of a motor unit, the basis of neural control of muscular activity.

MOTOR SKILL: A specific response for the accomplishment of a task (e.g., vertical jumping), which is learned through practice and depends on the presence of underlying motor abilities (e.g., kinesthetic sense).

MUSCLE SPINDLE: One of the mechanoreceptors arranged parallel to the fibers of skeletal muscle. It serves as the receptor of impulses responsible for the stretch reflex.

PROPRIOCEPTIVE FEEDBACK: Any of the sensory input concerning movements and the position of the body. It occurs chiefly in muscles, tendons and the labyrinth of the inner ear.

SENSORIMOTOR CORTEX: The part of the cerebral cortex concerned with the perception of sensory impulses and the generation of motor impulses.

SPINAL CORD: That part of the central nervous system lodged in the vertebral canal extending from the foramen magnum to the upper part of the lumbar region.

STRIATED MUSCLE CELLS: Any muscle whose fibers are divided by transverse bands into striations. Such muscles are voluntary (you must willfully move them).

SYNAPTIC JUNCTION: The area between the process of a neuron and the muscle fiber, which forms a place where a nervous impulse is transmitted from the neuron to the muscle fiber.

The literature indicates that other areas of the brain are also involved in the sequential pattern of muscle recruitment. These other areas, specifically the cerebellum and the basal ganglia, play a critical role in the initiation of a motor skill. As Table 2.2 illustrates, at least two different neural pathways are involved in performing a motor skill.

Table 2.2 Pathways of Thought for Motor Activities*

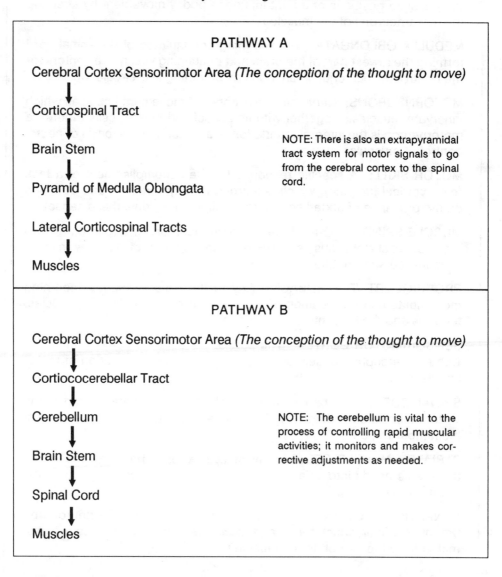

PATHWAY A

Cerebral Cortex Sensorimotor Area *(The conception of the thought to move)*

↓

Corticospinal Tract

↓

Brain Stem

↓

Pyramid of Medulla Oblongata

↓

Lateral Corticospinal Tracts

↓

Muscles

NOTE: There is also an extrapyramidal tract system for motor signals to go from the cerebral cortex to the spinal cord.

PATHWAY B

Cerebral Cortex Sensorimotor Area *(The conception of the thought to move)*

↓

Cortiococerebellar Tract

↓

Cerebellum

↓

Brain Stem

↓

Spinal Cord

↓

Muscles

NOTE: The cerebellum is vital to the process of controlling rapid muscular activities; it monitors and makes corrective adjustments as needed.

* Note: These are the initial pathways. Once an activity has been repeated many times, scientists agree that it is possible that the action is subsequently initiated in a different location in the brain.

A major neural pathway for initiating movement starts as you conceive (think about) the movement in your sensorimotor cortex (see pathway A in Table 2.2). Motor signals are then transmitted from your sensorimotor cortex directly to the anterior motor neurons of your spinal cord via the corticospinal tract. The corticospinal tract traverses the brain stem, the pyramid of the medulla oblongata and the lateral corticospinal tracts of your spinal cord to terminate in the interneurons, which are located in the spinal cord. It should be noted that as the motor signal is descending to your spinal cord, it is also going to your cerebellum, and the cerebellum may have some input to "fine tune" your coordination of movements (make corrective adjustments of the movements which are about to take place). The motor signal is finally transmitted to the muscle, which causes the muscle to contract.

Another neural route for the transmission of motor signals from the sensorimotor cortex involves the corticocerebellar tract (see pathway B in Table 2.2). This tract directs the motor signal from the sensorimotor cortex to the cortex of the cerebellum. The cerebellum has two critical roles involving movement. It helps you control rapid muscular movements and it enables you to make corrective adjustments in movements that were initiated in other areas of your brain. After entering the cerebellar cortex, the motor signal is then transmitted through the brain stem to the spinal cord. Finally, the muscles receive the motor signal from the spinal cord and respond accordingly.

No one is absolutely certain why one neural pathway is used over another or, for that matter, which route is actually used. To date, scientists have been unable to identify a precise command center for movements. What is known is that the two pathways are essential for producing movement.

A useful overview of the role your nervous system plays in initiating movement should also include an examination of the effect that sensory input has on learning a specific motor skill. Your body's sensory input mechanisms, in effect, allow you to memorize a motor skill, which results in your being able to perform that skill repeatedly (in a reasonably neurologically efficient manner).

Sensory input, referred to as proprioceptive feedback, is illustrated in Table 2.3. Sensory receptors transmit signals from your muscles, your skeletal joints and the areas surrounding the muscles to your cerebellum via the spinocerebellar tract. When a muscle contracts, muscle spindles (sensory organs located in your muscle), golgi tendon organs and joint receptors send information regarding the status of the muscular contraction, the degree of tension on the involved muscle tendon and the relative position of the extremity involved in the movement to your cerebellum. This information allows for the correction or adjustment of signals down the neural pathways to your muscles. As a result, you are able to achieve a more efficient movement pattern. Proprioceptive feedback enables you to figuratively "store" a pattern of the movement (e.g., the motor skill) in your motor system, as well as in your sensory system. Once the pattern is set, your body can perform the same movement repeatedly, with sensory input making adjustments of the skill only when necessary. After you have reached this point, you can conclude that you have "learned" the motor skill.

Table 2.3 Pathways of Proprioceptive Feedback

STRETCH RECEPTORS FOUND IN THE MUSCLE AREA

- MUSCLE SPINDLES (information on the relative length of the muscles)
- GOLGI TENDON ORGANS (information on the degree of tension on the muscle tendon)
- TACTILE TYPE RECEPTORS (information on the relative position of the body parts)

* Note: This feedback is transmitted via the ventral and dorsal spinocerebellar tracts.

CEREBELLUM

* Note: Adjustments are made via neural pathway B (see Table 2.2)

MUSCLES

Your decision to jump initiates the actions discussed in this section. The conception of the motor signal begins in your sensorimotor cortex and then travels down one of the aforementioned neural pathways to your spinal cord. In the spinal cord, the signal passes through interneurons and then moves out to your muscles via motor neurons. The motor neurons form synaptic junctions with striated muscle cells. Finally, the motor signal passes to the muscle cells and contraction occurs. And for one brief movement, you "soar" skyward. Table 2.4 provides a graphic overview of the process of neurological innervation of jumping.

Table 2.4 *Neuromuscular Involvement in Vertical Jumping*

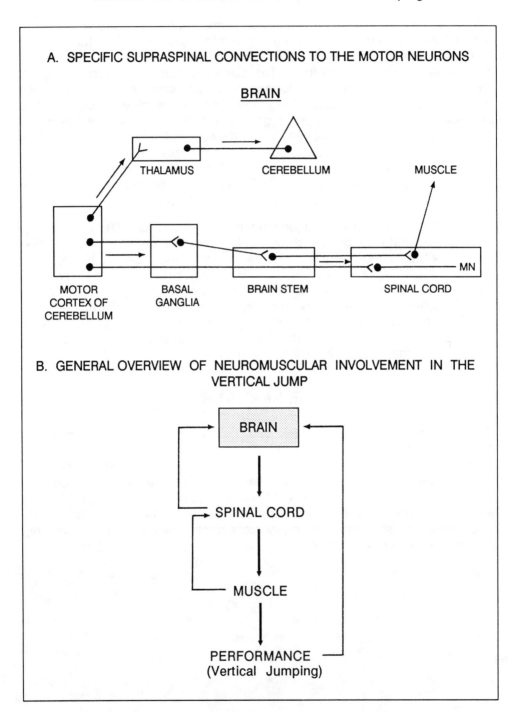

THE MUSCLES INVOLVED IN VERTICAL JUMPING

Vertical jumping involves two phases: preparing for the jump, and the upward lift of your body. During the preparation phase of the jump, your body is, in effect, "lowered" in an attempt to put the major muscles of your hip and thigh regions "on stretch." The muscle spindles, golgi tendon organs and other joint receptors send information to your brain, keeping it apprised of your body's position. Since the primary movement of your body in this phase involves lowering it against gravity, most (but not all) of the major muscles used in this movement are eccentrically contracted. The muscles involved in the preparation phase, the primary action of these muscles and the type of contraction each muscle undergoes are listed in Table 2.5. As you can see, the muscles are further categorized by degree of involvement: primary, secondary or stabilizers.

The second phase of vertical jumping involves the upward lift of your body. The muscles that were on stretch during the eccentric contraction of the first phase contract concentrically. The net effect is that your body applies a downward force against the ground. This, in turn, results in your body being "lifted" off the ground. All things being equal, the stronger your muscles, the more forceful the concentric contraction, and the more powerful the resultant lift. The literature refers to your upward momentum as the by-product of a kinetic summation of forces. Table 2.6 lists the muscles and the actions that occur during the upward lift phase of vertical jumping.

THE NEXT STEP

Part One of this text has focused on many of the fundamental considerations attendant to being able to jump higher: the role of vertical jumping in athletics, assessing your level of vertical jumping ability, comparing your level of jumping ability to others and understanding the mechanics of jumping. Part Two presents an easy-to-use guide to organizing an effective program for improving your ability to jump higher by developing your muscles (strength training), your stretch reflex (plyometric training) and your mind (mental training).

Table 2.5 The Musculature Involved in the Initial Phase of the Vertical Jump*

BODY PART →	MUSCLE →	MOVEMENT →	TYPE OF CONTRACTION
Trunk	Erector Spinal	Flexion	Eccentric
Shoulder Joint	Latissimus Dorsi Teres Major Posterior Deltoid Teres Minor Infraspinatus Triceps Brachii	Hyperextension	Concentric
Shoulder Girdle	Serratus Anterior Pectoralis Minor	Abduction	Concentric
Wrist	Wrist Extensors Wrist Flexors	Extension Flexion	Concentric Eccentric
Hip	Gluteus Medius Hamstrings	Flexion	Eccentric
	Gluteus Medius Gluteus Minimus	Slight Abduction	Concentric
Knee	Quadriceps	Flexion	Eccentric
Ankle	Tibialls Posterior Peroneus Longus Peroneus Brevis	Dorsiflexion	Eccentric

*Note: In the initial phase of the vertical jump, the primary muscles involved are the leg muscles, while the upper body muscles serve a secondary role. In this phase of the jump, the erector spinal muscles are the stabilizers.

Table 2.6 The Musculature Involved in the Upward Lift Phase of the Vertical Jump*

BODY PART →	MUSCLES →	MOVEMENT →	TYPE OF CONTRACTION
Trunk	Erector Spinal	Extension	Concentric
Shoulder Joint	Pectoralis Major Anterior Deltoid Biceps Brachii	Flexion	Concentric
Wrist	Wrist Extensors	Extension	Concentric
Hip	Gluteus Maximus Hamstrings Abductor Longus	Extension	Concentric
	Abductor Brevis Abductor Tertius Abductor Magnus	Abduction	Concentric
Knee	Quadriceps	Extension	Concentric
Ankle	Gastrocnemius Soleus Peroneus Longus Peroneus Brevis Tibialis Posterior	Plantar Flexion	Concentric

*Note: The muscles of the legs and the shoulder joint are of primary importance in the upward lift phase of the vertical jump. The wrist and trunk muscles serve a secondary role. At the top of the jump, the erector spinal muscles act as stabilizers.

PART TWO

IMPROVING YOUR VERTICAL JUMP

CHAPTER 3

STRENGTH TRAINING

The primary focus of any effort to effectively increase your ability to jump higher must be a sound strength training program. Adherence to a well-designed strength training program will enable you to jump higher because you will be able to exert more force in the muscles involved in vertical jumping. This improvement is a by-product of several adaptations that occur when you train properly. One of the adaptations is a larger percentage of fibers available for force production. In addition, these fibers will be able to contract more forcefully because of the presence of a higher concentration of contractile proteins. Other changes that occur as the result of proper training include: an increase in the number of myofibrils and capillaries per muscle fiber, an increase in the amount of connective tissue and more efficient energy utilization. The net result of these adaptations is that you will be able to jump higher.

Another desirable consequence of your efforts in the weight room is that, relatively speaking, you will be less susceptible to being injured while you participate in athletics. All other factors being equal, the more muscularly fit you are, the less likely you are to incur an injury. Several noted sports medicine physicians hypothesize that at least half of the injuries that occur in sports could have been prevented through a reasonable increase in overall muscular fitness. If that's the case, and we believe it is, then strength training is a fairly inexpensive and productive form of health insurance.

BASIC FUNDAMENTALS AND TECHNIQUES

Of the five basic components of physical fitness — aerobic fitness, flexibility, body leanness, muscular strength and muscular endurance — muscular fitness (the collective measure of muscular strength and muscular endurance) is the least understood by the scientific community. A number of factors can partially account for this situation. In the first place, strength training — the most common means by which higher levels of muscular fitness are attained — has often been viewed over the years as the exclusive pursuit of bodybuilders, Olympic lifters, overweight Russians, and would-be Arnold Schwarzenegger clones. It has only been in the last ten to fifteen years that strength training has gained general acceptance as a legitimate activity for all individuals interested in total fitness. Prior to this new-found concern with strength training, both the medical and the educational scientific communities dealt with the question of doing research in this area with a profound degree of disinterest. It may be a generalization, but it appears that prior to the mid-1970s, the typical attitude of potential investigators in this area was, *"Why bother?"*

Another probable reason for the lack of scientific information on muscular fitness has been the lack of precise measuring tools and acceptable investigative procedures that would enable investigators to accurately identify the basis and extent of any changes that occur in levels of muscular fitness. Forceplates, jerry-rigged dynamometers and Cybex equipment notwithstanding, the tools scientists need to measure change in muscular fitness with the degree of accuracy achieved in other physiological measurements simply do not exist. The usefulness of each of the currently most common means of assessing muscular fitness is somewhat limited. As a result, many investigators have chosen to focus their research efforts on other areas of human performance.

An additional factor that has limited researchers' interest in muscular fitness is the fact that, at best, it is very difficult to control all the factors influencing the subjects involved in strength training studies. Variances in subject motivation levels, eating habits, limb lengths, muscle lengths, percentage of fast- and slow-twitch muscle fibers and neurological efficiency levels are factors that can affect the results of any study examining the effects of selected strength training protocols. As a consequence, the literature is replete with strength training studies involving a limited number of subjects (often less than twelve), which attempt to extrapolate claims from results that do not lend themselves to such interpretation.

It is hardly surprising that strength training has held little scientific interest for most educators. Nor is it surprising, given the general information void relating to muscular fitness, that there are an almost unlimited number of contradictory and confusing theories on how to strength train in the athletic arena. As a coach or an athlete, you can easily be perplexed in trying to decide what to do in this area.

At West Point the dilemma facing us is often worse. We have to provide the best possible advice to every cadet seeking to improve performance or to rehabilitate an injury. If we do not do so, and the cadet is subsequently expelled because of a performance deficiency or a medical problem — either of which could have been resolved — then we haven't done our job. In dealing with the outstanding individuals at West Point, there simply is no alternative other than providing as sound advice as possible in every instance. The information presented in the following sections reflects our commitment to that principle.

WHAT EQUIPMENT SHOULD YOU USE?

Coaches and athletes frequently ask questions about the equipment that should be used while strength training. The answer is simple: Use the best tool you have available. Keep in mind that, within reason, it's not the tool you use, but the way you use the tool that determines the results you achieve. In general, there are two contradictory, but equally foolish, arguments advanced concerning equipment. The first states that the best and only way to train is to use free weights. If you don't, so the argument goes, you can't develop the balance and general body awareness that are an integral part of free weight workouts. The other position argues that only the most recently developed, high tech equipment will produce the best results.

Both arguments tend to be self-indulgent attempts to justify specific preferences. For your purposes, you should remember that the single thing you must do to achieve an increase in your level of muscular fitness is to place a demand on your system. The demand can come from a free weight, a Universal Gym machine (the generic name for a piece of equipment that has a pin-loaded weight stack and often has several stations as part of the same machine), a Nautilus machine (the generic name for variable resistance, direct resistance, muscle specific equipment) or even a sack of petrified cheeseburgers, as long as it places a demand on your system. You must consider a number of factors, including availability, cost, safety, time involved and effectiveness, and then make your decision on what equipment to use. There is little doubt that machines offer a safer, more efficient way to train. On the other hand, many coaches and athletes prefer free weights because of their relatively low cost and the wide range of angles that specific muscles can be exercised when using a free bar with an incline bench. These individuals also feel very comfortable with their perception of having to "control" the bar while lifting.

WHAT GUIDELINES SHOULD YOU FOLLOW?

Any listing of all the guidelines attendant to a sound strength training program would be highly subjective and somewhat boundless. Among the more important considerations and relevant principles are the following ten guidelines:

1. Base your strength training program, as much as possible, on scientific facts—not on intuition or on what this year's batch of championship athletes are doing. Keep in mind that many top athletes are champions not because of what they do, but in spite of it.

2. Adhere to the concept that maximum intensity will yield maximum results. Maximum intensity refers to the idea of working to a point of not being able to perform an exercise through a full range of motion in both the concentric (lifting) and the eccentric (lowering) phases of the exercise. This point is also sometimes referred to as the point of momentary muscular failure. If you don't reach this point, it does not mean you won't get positive results—you just won't achieve what you could have if you had reached that point.

3. Follow the concept that your program must be progressive in nature. Too much, too soon will lead to either an injury or failure, or both. You should gradually increase the stresses you impose upon your muscles as they reach a point where they are able to accommodate a particular demand.

4. Emphasize the concept of specificity in your program. There is only one proper way to perform a specific exercise. If you compromise the mechanics of an exercise, you will compromise the results achieved by performing that exercise. Learn how to perform each exercise and then take steps to insure that you do the exercises properly. The latter goal is best achieved by working out with a partner who has both an excellent knowledge of how to perform the exercise and the personal temperament required to make you train correctly. Specificity also involves selecting the right exercise to develop a specific muscle. If you want to develop a specific area of your body, you need to know what exercises will help you achieve your goal.

5. Perform every exercise through a full range of motion. If you don't go through a full range of motion, you will eventually suffer a decrease in your level of flexibility (specific to the joint[s] involved in the exercise), as well as perform less work. Since the distance over which a muscle moves a weight is proportional to the amount of work that is done (WORK = FORCE X DISTANCE), you will perform less work if you decrease the distance you move the weight.

6. Perform every exercise at a controlled rate of speed. If you raise and lower a weight in a relatively slow manner (approximately two seconds to execute the concentric phase and three to four seconds to do the eccentric phase), your muscles will be performing work throughout the entire exercise. If you do the exercise in an explosive manner (e.g., if you throw or jerk the weight), your muscles actually will be working only at the beginning (rapidly accelerating) and at the end (rapidly decelerating) of the lift. No work is performed in the mid-range of the lift. In addition, the rapid deceleration involved in throwing a weight is likely to cause an injury to the lifter.

7. Develop a program that emphasizes muscle balance. In your body you have muscles that oppose each other (e.g., your quadricep muscles are opposed by your hamstring muscles). These muscles have a proportional strength relationship between them. If one is too strong for the other, you run the risk of injury to the disproportionally weaker muscle. For maximum results, you must organize a program that emphasizes the principle of working these antagonistic muscles.

8. Understand that your mind will play an integral role, not only in how much you lift, but also in the results you actually achieve from your strength training program. Some practitioners theorize that you lift a weight almost as much with your mind as you do with your muscles. Accordingly, keep your program relatively simple. As a general rule, for example, no overriding reason exists for following any breathing technique when you are lifting except for, "Don't hold your breath." The techniques you adhere to while lifting weights should become instinctive, so that no mental energy will have to be expended on any goal other than reaching a true point of muscular fatigue on each exercise.

9. Know the misconceptions attendant to strength training so that your goal expectations are realistically set and your program efforts are rationally directed. For example, many male athletes not only want to be able to jump higher, but also to add ten to fifteen pounds of muscle. Given the realities of how and why individuals are able to gain muscle mass, such an expectation is beyond attainment for all women and most men. When they do not achieve their goal of developing additional muscle mass, many athletes quickly look for another strength training program to adopt. More failure follows, and a counterproductive cycle is set in motion. Another misconception frequently espoused by members of the strength training community is the belief that the taking of certain dietary supplements (e.g., protein or amino acid tablets) will somehow facilitate the development of muscle tissue. This belief is simply not true. Keep in mind that proper strength training is hard work. Knowing how to structure

a proper strength training program, and knowing what will and will not be the consequences of participating in such a program will produce much better results for you in the long run.

10. Focus on the concept of *arete.* The Greek genesis of the word "aristocrat," *arete* literally means "to be the best you can be." By focusing on *arete,* your chances of avoiding the often destructively competitive attitudes of individuals who lift weight will be improved. These individuals place great stock in how much they lift, as opposed to the way they should lift. More often than not, their misplaced focus leads to failure, injury, or lessened results. You should not worry about what other individuals can lift. Often any difference between the two of you on a specific exercise is due to factors beyond your control (e.g., limb length, hormonal levels).

WHAT PROGRAM SHOULD YOU ADOPT?

It would not be an exaggeration to say that literally hundreds of different strength training programs currently are in use by athletes in the United States. Accepting the fact that no one would willingly engage in a program that doesn't work, it is fairly safe to surmise that all of these programs increase muscular fitness — if for no other reason than they all place a demand on the muscular systems of the athletes who follow them. In the face of this, how, then, can you select a strength training program that will best meet your needs? You must first decide what your needs are and what factors affect your ability to meet these needs. Next, you must identify a program that will — given the limiting situational factors facing you — permit you to achieve your program objectives.

For the cadets at West Point (as well as for most people, we conclude), these needs can be grouped into three general goals. We want to achieve as much as we can from our program (effectiveness), as quickly as we can (efficiency), and as injury-free as possible (safety). All possible programs are judged against these three considerations. If the criteria you hold important are different than ours, somewhere along the line you will be forced to decide to what degree you are willing to compromise effectiveness, efficiency and safety for other considerations.

Once you've decided what goals your program should achieve, you must then design a program to meet those goals. All programs, even the constantly changing ones advocated by the wide range of "freak-of-the-week" muscle magazines, tend to fall into two groups: multi-set programs (the traditional approach) and single-set programs (the so-called H.I.T. theory — High Intensity Training). There is wide and often acrimonious disagreement among strength training practitioners regarding which approach will produce the greatest gains. Choosing a program is something that is best left to each individual. At West Point we (as a general rule, not as a matter of formal policy or institutional endorsement) have successfully followed the H.I.T. theory of strength training since 1975.

Regardless of the training philosophy you ascribe to, designing a strength training program involves dealing with seven basic variables. In general, both major philosophies of strength development are in basic concurrence with four of the seven variables. Major philosophical differences exist, however, on the three variables involving the numbers part of the program recipe for developing strength: reps, sets and weight (resistance). The seven variables are examined below with any critical differences between the traditional philosophy of training and the H.I.T. theory noted.

Variable #1. How many exercises should be performed? In general, a workout should be limited to twelve to fourteen exercises. These exercises should consist of a core set of ten exercises designed to develop the five major muscle groups in your body (lower back and buttocks, legs, torso, arms and abdominals), plus two to four exercises selected to meet specific individual or program needs (e.g., neck exercises for football players, abductor-adductor exercises for individuals who are prone to groin pulls). The last two sections of this chapter describe specific strength training exercises that you should perform to increase your vertical jumping ability. In addition, several sample strength training programs are offered to enable you to achieve that goal.

Variable #2. In what order whould you perform the exercises? In general, all strength training should be done beginning with those exercises involving the largest muscles and proceeding to those involving the smallest muscles. The basis for this guideline is the fact that all strength training exercises are designed primarily to develop the largest muscle involved in the exercise. If you have to quit performing an exercise because a smaller muscle is fatigued before the larger one, then you've compromised the possible gains from your program.

Variables #3, #4 and #5.* How many repetitions of an exercise should you perform? How many sets of an exercise should you do? How much weight (resistance) should you lift? These variables constitute the numbers crunch of strength training. In the world of athletics, the variances in the protocols adopted to purportedly develop strength are extraordinarily diverse. The traditional approach to strength training (based on the progressive resistance theories advanced by noted exercise physiologist T. L. DeLorme) suggests that a proper strength development program consists of three sets of five to eight repetitions for developing strength and three sets of nine to fifteen repetitions for

* A repetition is doing a specific exercise one time. A set is doing so many repetitions in a row before you stop. The weight used is the level of resistance (demand) you place on your muscles by attempting to lift that amount.

developing endurance. Proponents of this approach recommend either selecting a weight that will enable you to perform all sets at a point somewhere between the suggested minimum and maximum number of repetitions before reaching muscular failure, or selecting a weight based on the one-max rep system. The one-max rep system is based on first determining the maximum amount you can lift in a single repetition of a specific exercise and then lifting a (highly) arbitrary percentage of that amount on each specific set of that exercise.

Proponents of high intensity training would argue that the traditional arbitrary and subjective manipulation of a program's numbers is nothing more than an attempt to add a degree of numerical mystique (and hence scientific creditability) to an individual's strength training efforts. H.I.T. advocates follow a philosophy that "more is not better." These individuals claim that once you recruit as many muscle fibers as you are going to recruit in a strength training workout, additional work is, at best, a waste of time and possibly may be counterproductive. The H.I.T. protocol recommends performing one set of eight to twelve repetitions to muscular failure, regardless of whether or not you are interested in developing muscular strength or muscular endurance. The weight lifted should be an amount that will permit you to perform at least eight, but not more than twelve, repetitions of an exercise. You should increase the amount lifted when you are able to perform twelve repetitions. If you cannot do at least eight repetitions of the exercise at the increased weight, either you increased the weight too much, or your last workout (or this workout) gave you a false indication of your actual level of muscular fitness. Individuals who adhere to the high intensity training approach would argue that most individuals do not have a constant, measurable maximum level of strength. Rather, your mental state on a given day can greatly affect how much you can lift. If you're "up," you often feel like you could lift the world. If you're "down," you probably will feel like every weight is somehow attached to a Wurlitzer piano. Unfortunately, it is sometimes very difficult to determine what mental state you're in. If you perform every exercise to the best of your ability and strictly adhere to sound training guidelines, the concept of *arete* will govern your results.

Variable #6. How much time should you take between exercises in your program? In order to achieve a measure of administrative efficiency in the weight room, it is recommended that you limit the time between exercises to less than one minute. There is no science involved here, just sound time management. Minimize the standing around. Maximize the flow pattern of those using the strength training facility. Get in and get out with a minimum amount of chaos and waste of time.

Variable #7. How much time should you take between workouts? Unless you are engaged in a split workout routine (upper body exercises one day, lower body exercises the next day), it is recommended that you allow at least two days, but not more than four days, between workouts. An alternate-day regimen (*Monday–Wednesday–Friday* or *Tuesday–Thursday–Saturday)* is the most commonly followed system.

On the following two pages is a chart (Table 3.1) listing four different methods used to improve the vertical jump: free weight exercises, Universal gym exercises, Nautilus exercises, and partner resistance exercises.   Any listing of strength training exercises is, at best, subjective and most likely incomplete.   The exercises listed in Table 3.1 and detailed in the remainder of this chapter offer a representative, but not inclusive, program for improving vertical jumping ability.

Table 3.1 Strength Training Exercises for Improving Vertical Jumping Ability

LOWER BODY MUSCLES	EXERCISES			
	FREE WEIGHTS	UNIVERSAL	NAUTILUS	PR EXERCISES
ERECTOR SPINAE	Squat Bent-legged Dead Lift Stiff-legged Dead Lift Good Morning Power High Pull	Back Extension	Hip Extension	BackMate® Squat Back Extension
BUTTOCKS	Squat Bent-legged Dead Lift Leg Press (AMF) Lunge Jump Squat Step Up Stiff-legged Dead Lift	Leg Press	Hip Extension Leg Press Hip Abduction	BackMate® Squat Leg Press Hip Abduction
QUADRICEPS	Squat Bent-legged Dead Lift Leg Press (AMF) Lunge Jump Squat Step Up Power High Pull Power Clean	Leg Extension Leg Press	Leg Extension Leg Press Hip Abduction	Leg Press
HAMSTRINGS	Squat Stiff-legged Dead Lift Leg Press (AMF) Lunge	Leg Curl	Leg Curl	Leg Curl Squat
HIP FLEXORS	Step Up			Hip Flexion
HIP EXTENSORS	Squat Power High Pull Power Clean			
CALVES	Heel Raise Stiff-legged Dead Lift Power High Pull Power Clean	Heel Raise	Heel Raise	Heel Raise
ADDUCTOR MAGNUS			Hip Adduction	Hip Adduction

UPPER BODY MUSCLES	EXERCISES			
	FREE WEIGHTS	UNIVERSAL	NAUTILUS	PR EXERCISES
DELTOIDS	Upright Row Bench Press	Upright Row Bench Press	Arm Cross Rowing Torso	Bent-arm Fly Front Raise Bent-over Side Lateral Raise Seated Press Back Pulldown
TRAPEZIUS	Power High Pull Power Clean Upright Row Shoulder Shrug	Upright Row Shoulder Shrug	Shoulder Shrug	Shoulder Shrug Bent-over Side Lateral Raise
ROTATOR CUFF				Internal Rotation External Rotation
RHOMBOIDS	Bent-over Fly		Rowing Torso	Back Pulldown Bent-over Side Lateral Raise
LATISSIMUS DORSI	Chin-up Bent-over Rowing Bent-over Fly	Lat Pulldown	Chin-up Pullover	Lat Pulldown
PECTORALS	Bench Press	Bench Press	Arm Cross	Bench Press Bent-arm Fly Front Raise
BICEPS	Chin-up Bent-over Rowing Bicep Curl Power High Pull Power Clean	Upright Row Bicep Curl Lat Pulldown	Chin-up Two-arm Curl	Bicep Curl Lat Pulldown Back Pulldown
TRICEPS	French Curl Bench Press	Tricep Extension Bench Press	Tricep Extension	Tricep Extension Bench Press Seated Press
FOREARM EXTENSORS/ FLEXORS	Wrist Curl Reverse Wrist Curl	Wrist Curl Reverse Wrist Curl	Wrist Curl Reverse Wrist Curl	

* Note: The power clean, the power high pull, and the jump squat are fairly popular, yet highly dangerous exercises. The authors caution athletes to strictly adhere to proper techniques while performing these exercises.

FREE WEIGHT EXERCISES

Squat

Muscles used: Major muscles of the legs, buttocks

Starting position: Stand with your feet approximately shoulder width apart and the barbell resting on your upper back. Do not lock out your legs.

Description: Lower your buttocks until the middle of your thigh is parallel to the floor and recover to the starting position.

Points to emphasize:
- Keep your head up and your back straight throughout the movement.
- Do not bounce at the bottom of the movement.
- Heel supports, such as $2^{1}/_{2}$ lb. plates, may be used until ankle flexibility increases.
- Since this exercise begins with the negative movement, always use spotters.

starting position

mid-range position

Free Weight Exercises: Bent-legged Dead Lift

Muscles used: Spinal erectors, gluteus maximus, quadriceps

Starting position: Stand with your feet slightly more than shoulder width apart. Squat and grip the bar with an underhand grip with your non-dominant hand and an overhand grip with your dominant hand. Keep your elbows outside your knees and your head up.

Description: Pull the bar while straightening your legs and your back until you are standing straight with your shoulders back. Then pause, slowly recover to the starting position and repeat.

Points to emphasize:
- Keep your back straight and lift with your legs.
- Keep the bar close to your shins throughout the exercise.
- Roll your shoulders back at the completion of the positive movement.

starting position   *mid-range position*

Free Weight Exercises: Stiff-legged Dead Lift

Muscles used: Lower back, hamstrings, buttocks, calves

Starting position: Place your feet approximately shoulder width apart (no wider). In the standing position, take the bar in your hand with an alternate grip.

Description: Bend at the waist and lower the weight to its lowest possible point. Hang a few seconds and then return to the starting position.

Points to emphasize:
- Keep your legs locked.
- Lower the weight slowly.
- If the weight touches the floor, stand on a higher platform.
- Never bounce.

starting position

mid-range position

Free Weight Exercises: Leg Press (AMF)

Muscles used: Quadriceps, buttocks, hamstrings

Starting position: Lie on your back with your shoulders against the pad, your feet on the foot bar, your hands on the hand holders and your knees up against your body.

Description: Extend your legs until they are almost fully extended (do not lock out—this allows your legs time to recover and puts pressure on the joints). Slowly return your legs to the starting position. Do not bounce because this will shorten the actual time the muscle is working.

Points to emphasize:
- Relax your upper body.
- Do not use your hands on your knees to assist.
- Do not apply pressure to your other body parts.
- Do not hold your breath.

starting position

mid-range position

Free Weight Exercises: Lunge

Muscles used: Quadriceps, buttocks, hamstrings

Starting position: The bar should rest across the trapezius and the back of your shoulders. Your feet should be comfortably together, and your head should remain erect.

Description: Stride forward with one leg. Lower your body so that the upper (front) leg is parallel to the ground and the trail leg is slightly extended. The knee should gently touch the floor. Push back with the front leg, keeping the trunk erect, and return to the starting position. Alternate legs. Try to push with enough force to prevent the heel from dragging on the floor.

Points to emphasize:
- Caution should be used when first beginning this lift.
- Start with a light weight, learn the movement and gradually increase the work load.

starting position

mid-range position

Free Weight Exercises: Jump Squat

Muscles used: Quadriceps, buttocks

Starting position: The bar should rest on your shoulders as in the squat exercise. One of your legs should be placed slightly in front of the other.

Description: Lower the weight $1/4$ depth and jump, exploding with the weight upward. At the same time, reverse the foot position. A weight lifting belt should be worn for lower back support. Begin this exercise with a light weight. Learn the movement and increase the load once a base strength level has been developed.

starting position

mid-range position

(switch the position of your feet and body while jumping)

Free Weight Exercises: Step Up

Muscles used: Quadriceps, buttocks, hip flexors

Starting position: The bar should rest across your trapezius and shoulders, as in the squat exercise. Your feet should be in a comfortable position.

Description: Beginning with your right leg, step up onto a bench or blocks and lift your body with that leg. Drive the knee of the trail leg up. Slowly lower your body by stepping down one leg at a time. Repeat, alternating lead legs.

Points to emphasize:
  • Do not bounce.

starting position   *begin by stepping up*   *mid-range position*
                             on one foot

Free Weight Exercises: Good Morning

Muscles used: Back, sacrospinalis

Starting position: Place the bar across your shoulders. Your feet should be more than shoulder width apart. Keep your head up, your shoulders back and your back tight.

Description: Bend forward at the waist, stopping when your chest is parallel to the ground. Straighten to the starting position. Keep your neck pulled against the bar and your shoulders back. Wear a weight lifting belt for lower back support. Use a light weight and progress slowly when beginning this lift.

Points to emphasize:
- Do not hyperextend your back (do not extend your back past your hips while recovering to the starting position).

starting position

mid-range position

Free Weight Exercises: Heel Raise

Muscles used: Calves

Starting position: Stand with your toes on a piece of wood or on a barbell plate and place the barbell behind your neck on your shoulders.

Description: Raise your heels up as high as possible, pause, and lower them back to the starting position. Upon touching the floor, immediately raise your heels again. Allow no time for rest or recovery.

Points to emphasize:
  • In the starting position, your toes are in a position higher than your heels.

starting position

mid-range position

Free Weight Exercises: Bent-over Rowing

Muscles used: Latissimus dorsi, biceps

Starting position: Stand with your feet shoulder width apart and your knees slightly bent. Bend forward at the waist until your torso is parallel to the floor. Grip the bar with an overhand grip with your hands more than shoulder width apart.

Description: Raise the bar to the center of your chest, pause, then slowly lower the bar to the starting position and repeat.

Points to emphasize:
- Keep your head up and your back straight.
- Keep your back parallel to the floor.

starting position

mid-range position

Free Weight Exercises: Power High Pull

Muscles used: Trapezius, biceps, quadriceps, calves, hip extensors, lower back, upper back

Starting position: With the bar lying on the floor, squat down to the bar, keeping your buttocks underneath you and your back straight. Then grip the bar in an overhand fashion at about shoulder width. Your head should be up, and your feet should be about ten to twelve inches apart.

Description: From the starting position, start the bar moving by extending your legs. Once the bar reaches about knee level, you should extend explosively and completely from the knee, hip and ankle joints while pulling the bar upward in a path that is straight and close to your body. This pull starts with an explosive shrugging action and concludes with an upward pulling action of your arms. You should pull the bar to eye level or higher, and then you should return the bar to the starting position. The bar is not turned over on the top of the pull as in the power clean lift.

Points to emphasize:
- Pull the bar in a straight upward path that is close to your body.
- The legs and hips work initially to start the bar moving.
- The arms come into play after your legs and hips have caused the bar to accelerate.
- The elbows should be high and to the side during the pull.
- Don't pull prematurely with your arms.
- Explosiveness in the legs and hips is the critical factor.
- If available, a spotter should be used.

starting position

mid-range position

Free Weight Exercises: Power Clean*

Muscles used: Trapezius, biceps, quadriceps, calves, hip extensors, lower
   back, upper back

Starting position: With the bar lying on the floor, squat down to the bar,
   keeping your buttocks underneath you and your back straight. Then grip
   the bar in an overhand fashion at about shoulder width. Your head should
   be up, and your feet should be about ten to twelve inches apart.

Description: From the starting position, start the bar moving by extending
   your legs. Once the weight is at about knee level, extend explosively and
   completely from the knee, hip and ankle joints while pulling the bar
   vertically in a straight line.   This pull starts as an explosive shrugging
   action and concludes with an upward pulling action of your arms. Once
   the bar is pushed (legs, hips) and pulled (trapezius, biceps) to its highest
   point, simply drop under the bar to catch it.

Points to emphasize:
   • Pull the weight upward in a straight line.
   • Utilize the large, powerful muscles initially (legs, hips).
   • Finish the lift with the smaller, weaker muscles (arms).
   • Keep your elbows high and to the sides during the pull.
   • Explosiveness from the legs and hips is the critical factor.
   • If available, spotters should be used.

---

*   This exercise should not be used until you have mastered the pulling technique of the power
    high pull exercise.

starting position

mid-range position

Free Weight Exercises: Chin-up

Muscles used: Latissimus dorsi, biceps

Starting position: Grip the bar with an underhand grip, your hands shoulder width apart. Hang from the bar with your elbows straight.

Description: Raise your body until your chin is above the bar, pause, then slowly recover to the starting position and repeat.

Points to emphasize:
- Do not allow your body to swing during the exercise. Allow your elbows to extend completely at the bottom of the movement.

starting position

mid-range position

Free Weight Exercises: Shoulder Shrug

Muscles used: Trapezius

Starting position: Stand with your feet shoulder width apart and your arms extended downward. Grip the bar with an overhand grip with your hands shoulder width apart.

Description: Keeping your arms straight, raise your shoulders as high as possible, pause, then slowly recover to the starting position and repeat.

Points to emphasize:
- Stand straight throughout the exercise.
- Allow your shoulders to drop as far as possible at the bottom of the movement.

starting position   *mid-range position*

Free Weight Exercises: Upright Row

Muscles used: Deltoids, trapezius

Starting position: Stand with your feet shoulder width apart and your arms extended downward. Grip the bar with an overhand grip with your hands less than shoulder width apart.

Description: Pull the bar upward without bending your torso until the bar touches your chin, pause, then slowly recover to the starting position and repeat.

Points to emphasize:
- Stand straight with your head up throughout the exercise.
- Pull the bar all the way to your chin.

starting position

mid-range position

Free Weight Exercises: Bent-over Fly

Muscles used: Latissimus dorsi, rhomboids

Starting position: Stand with your feet shoulder width apart and your knees slightly bent. Bend forward at the waist until your torso is parallel to the floor. Grip the dumbbells with your palms facing inward, arms straight and the dumbbells touching each other.

Description: Raise your arms laterally as high as possible, pause, then slowly recover to the starting position and repeat.

Points to emphasize:
- Keep your head up and your back straight.
- Keep your back parallel to the floor throughout the exercise.

starting position   *mid-range position*

Free Weight Exercises: Bench Press

Muscles used: Pectorals, deltoids, triceps

Starting position: Lie flat on the bench with your buttocks and the backs of
   your shoulders flat on the bench. Bend your knees and place your feet
   flat on the floor. Grip the bar with your hands slightly more than shoulder
   width apart.

Description: Lower the bar to the center of your chest. Pause, then push
   your arms upward until your elbows are extended and repeat.

Points to emphasize:
   • Do not raise your buttocks off the bench.
   • Do not bounce the weight off your chest.
   • Exhale while raising the weight.
   • When using a near maximum weight, utilize spotters.

starting position

mid-range position

Free Weight Exercises: Bicep Curl

Muscles used: Biceps

Starting position: Sit on a bench with your arms extended downward and resting on a pad. Grip the bar with an underhand grip.

Description: Keep your elbows back and curl the bar as high as possible, pause, then slowly recover to the starting position and repeat.

Points to emphasize:
- Keep your back straight (do not lean back).
- Keep your elbows back throughout the exercise.

starting position

mid-range position

Free Weight Exercises: French Curl

Muscles used: Triceps

Starting position: Lie flat on the bench with your knees bent and your feet flat on the floor. Grip the bar with an overhand grip with your hands less than shoulder width apart. Your upper arms should be perpendicular to the floor with the bar just above your forehead.

Description: Extend your arms upward until your elbows are straight. Pause, then slowly recover to the starting position and repeat.

Points to emphasize:
- Keep your upper arms perpendicular to the floor throughout the exercise.
- Keep your elbows shoulder width apart throughout the exercise.

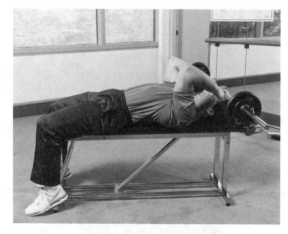

starting position

mid-range position

Free Weight Exercises: Wrist Curl

Muscles used: Forearm flexors

Starting position: Sit on the end of an exercise bench with your forearms resting on your thighs. Grip the bar with an underhand grip and allow your wrists to bend downward.

Description: Curl the bar up toward your elbows as far as possible. Pause, then slowly recover to the starting position and repeat.

Points to emphasize:
- Keep your forearms flat on your thighs throughout the exercise.
- Keep your wrists just over the ends of your knees.

starting position

mid-range position

Free Weight Exercises: Reverse Wrist Curl

Muscles used: Forearm extensors

Starting position: Sit on the end of the bench with your knees bent and your feet flat on the floor. Place your forearms firmly against your thighs. Grip the bar with an overhand grip and allow your wrists to bend downward.

Description: Curl your wrists up and back as far as possible, pause, then slowly recover to the starting position and repeat.

Points to emphasize:
- Keep your forearms in contact with your thighs throughout the exercise.
- Keep your wrists just over the ends of your knees.

starting position   *mid-range position*

UNIVERSAL GYM EXERCISES

Leg Press

Muscles used: Gluteus maximus, quadriceps

Starting position: Sit with your shoulders against the seat back with the balls of your feet centered on the foot pads. Adjust the seat so that your knee joints are at less than a ninety degree angle. Loosely grip the handles.

Description: Straighten both of your legs, but do not lock out because that would allow your thigh muscles to relax. Pause, then slowly recover to the starting position and repeat.

Points to emphasize:
- Do not grip the handles tightly.
- Do not bounce the weight stack at the bottom of the movement.

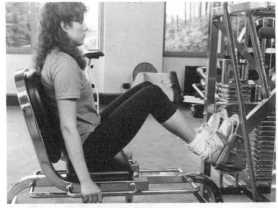

starting position

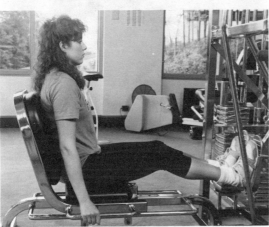

mid-range position

Universal Gym Exercises: Leg Extension

Muscles used: Quadriceps

Starting position: In a seated position, place both of your feet behind the roller pads with the backs of your knees against the front of the seat. Keep your head and shoulders in a vertical position throughout the exercise.

Description: Raise your feet until both your legs are straight. Pause, then slowly recover to the starting position and repeat.

Points to emphasize:
- Grip the sides of the bench loosely with your hands.
- Keep your hands, neck and face muscles relaxed during the exercise.

starting position

mid-range position

Universal Gym Exercises: Leg Curl

Muscles used: Hamstrings

Starting position: Lie face down on the bench. Place the backs of your ankles under the roller pads with your kneecaps just off the end of the bench.

Description: Curl your legs upward as far as possible. Pause, then slowly recover to the starting position and repeat.

Points to emphasize:
- Your feet should be in a flexed position with your toes pointing toward your knees.
- In the contracted position, your lower legs should be perpendicular to the bench or even further back.

starting position

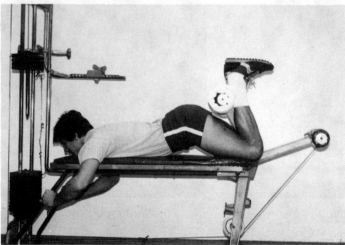

mid-range position

Universal Gym Exercises: Heel Raise

Muscles used: Calves

Starting position: Stand facing the weight stack. Grip the handles with an overhand grip and raise the weights to the level of your shoulders. Place the balls of your feet on a block of wood.

Description: Elevate your heels as high as possible. Pause, then slowly recover to the starting position and repeat.

Points to emphasize:
- Do not let your heels touch the ground.
- Do not bend your knees.

starting position

mid-range position

Universal Gym Exercises: Back Extension

Muscles used: Back muscles, sacrospinalis

Starting position: Firmly place your feet on the roller pad and pedal. Support your hips or stomach on the padded bar. Place your hands behind your head.

Description: From a hanging position, lift your head and trunk to a position parallel to your hips. Weight can be held behind your head for greater resistance.

Points to emphasize:
- Do not exercise to failure.
- Build the work load gradually.
- Be careful not to overwork your back in your initial workouts.
- Do not hyperextend your back in the mid-range position of the exercise.

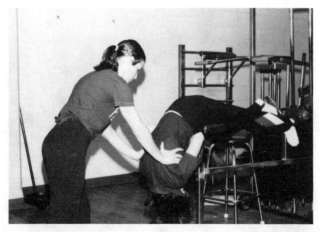

starting position

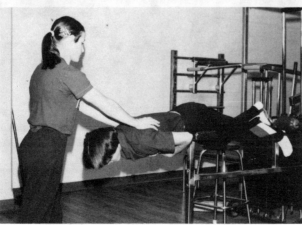

mid-range position

Universal Gym Exercises: Lat Pulldown

Muscles used: Latissimus dorsi, biceps

Starting position: Assume a kneeling position facing the weight stack. Grip the curved handles on the bar.

Description: Pull the bar down and touch the base of your neck. Pause, then slowly recover to the starting position and repeat.

Points to emphasize:
- A sitting position may be used if preferred.
- A closer grip may be used to place more emphasis on your biceps.

starting position   *mid-range position*

Universal Gym Exercises: Shoulder Shrug

Muscle used: Trapezius

Starting position: Stand between the bench press handles facing the weight stack. Grip the insides of the handles with an overhand grip.

Description: Keep your arms straight and raise your shoulders as high as possible. Pause, then slowly recover to the starting position and repeat.

Points to emphasize:
- Keep your body perfectly straight.
- Allow your arms to drop as far as possible on the negative movement without bending your back.

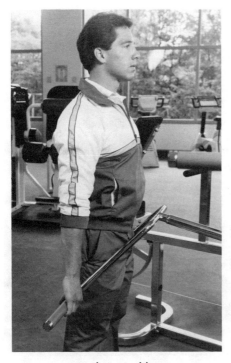
starting position

mid-range position

Universal Gym Exercises: Upright Row

Muscles used: Trapezius, deltoids, biceps

Starting position: Stand facing the bicep curl station and grip the handles with an overhand grip with your hands less than shoulder width apart.

Description: Pull the bar up until it touches the underside of your chin. Pause, then slowly recover to the starting position and repeat.

Points to emphasize:
- Stand straight with your head up throughout the exercise.
- Keep your elbows pointed to the outside.
- Pull the bar all the way to your chin.

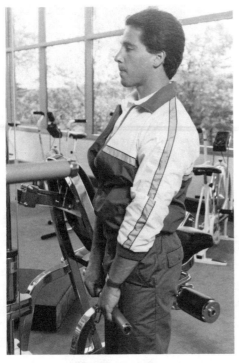

starting position

mid-range position

Universal Gym Exercises: Bench Press

Muscles used: Pectorals, deltoids, triceps

Starting position: Lie flat on the bench with your knees bent and your feet flat on the floor. Adjust the bench so that the handles are aligned with the center of your chest. Grip the handles using an overhand grip with your hands slightly more than shoulder width apart.

Description: Straighten your arms until your elbows are fully extended. Pause, then slowly recover to the starting position and repeat.

Points to emphasize:
- A block of wood may be placed under the head of the bench for greater range of movement.
- Do not arch your back.
- Do not bounce the weight stack at the bottom.
- Exhale while raising the weight.

starting position

mid-range position

Universal Gym Exercises: Bicep Curl

Muscles used: Biceps

Starting position: Stand with your arms extended downward facing the bicep curl station. Grip the bar using an underhand grip with your hands shoulder width apart.

Description: Curl the bar forward and upward, keeping your elbows back until the bar touches the base of your neck. Pause, then slowly recover to the starting position and repeat.

Points to emphasize:
- Do not allow your elbows to come forward.
- Do not lean back during the exercise.

starting position   *mid-range position*

Universal Gym Exercises: Tricep Extension

Muscles used: Triceps

Starting position: Stand facing the pulldown station with your feet shoulder width apart. Grip the bar with an overhand grip with your hands less than shoulder width apart. Pull the bar down until your elbows are at your sides.

Description: Push your hands down until your arms are extended. Pause, then slowly recover to the starting position and repeat.

Points to emphasize:
- Your elbows should be kept at your sides.
- Wrapping your thumbs over the bar makes it easier to stabilize your wrists.
- For greater range of movement, wrap a towel around the cable junction of the bar, gripping both sides of the towel, and extend the towel downward.

starting position

mid-range position

Universal Gym Exercises: Wrist Curl

Muscles used: Forearm flexors

Starting position: Sit on the end of an exercise bench with your forearms resting on your knees. Grasp the handles with an underhand grip and raise the bar until the weight stack is lifted. Allow the handles to rest on your fingertips.

Description: Curl the bar up toward your elbows as far as possible. Pause, then slowly recover to the starting position and repeat.

Points to emphasize:
- Keep your forearms flat on your thighs throughout the exercise.
- Your wrists should be just over the ends of your knees.

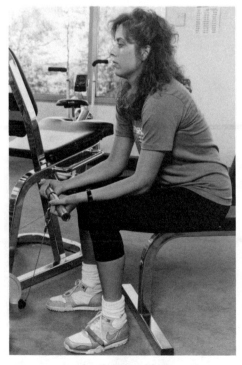

starting position

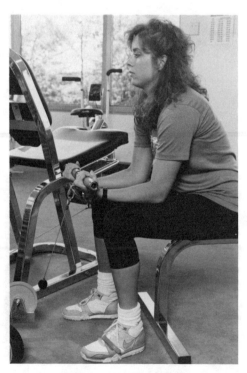

mid-range position

Universal Gym Exercises: Reverse Wrist Curl

Muscles used: Forearm extensors

Starting position: Sit on the end of an exercise bench with your forearms resting on your knees. Grasp the handles with an overhand grip.

Description: Curl the bar up toward your elbows as far as possible. Pause, then slowly recover to the starting position and repeat.

Points to emphasize:
- Keep your forearms flat on your thighs throughout the exercise.
- Your wrists should be just over the ends of your knees.

starting position

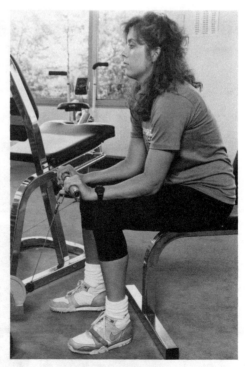

mid-range position

NAUTILUS EXERCISES

Hip Extension

Muscles used: Gluteus maximus, spinal erectors

Starting position: Lie on your back with your legs over the roller pads. Align your hip joints with the center of the rotation cams. Fasten the seat belt snugly around your waist and grasp the handles lightly. Extend both of your legs at the same time and push back with your hands.

Description: Hold one leg in the fully extended position and allow the other leg to bend up and back as far as possible. Extend your bent leg forward until it is even with your extended leg. Arch your lower back and force both legs downward. Pause, then repeat the same action with your other leg.

Points to emphasize:
- When your legs are fully extended in the contracted position, keep your knees straight and together and point your toes down.
- When one leg is bending back in the negative movement, do not allow your extended leg to raise up.

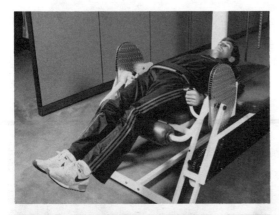

starting position

mid-range position

Nautilus Exercises: Leg Extension

Muscles used: Quadriceps

Sarting position: In a seated position, place both of your feet behind the roller pads with the backs of your knees against the front of the seat. Adjust the seat back so that it touches your lower back.

Description: Raise your feet until both of your legs are straight. Pause, then recover to the starting position and repeat. Keep your head and shoulders against the seat back throughout the exercise.

Points to emphasize:
- Move immediately from this exercise to the leg press exercise.
- Keep your hand, neck and face muscles relaxed during the exercise.

starting position

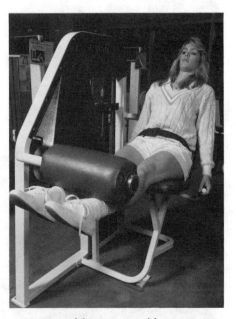

mid-range position

Nautilus Exercises: Leg Press

Muscles used: Gluteus maximus, quadriceps

Starting position: Flip the foot pads down. Place your feet on the pads with your toes turned slightly inward.

Description: Push both of your legs outward until your knees are straight. Pause with your knees slightly bent, then slowly recover to the starting position and repeat.

Points to emphasize:
- Move immediately from the leg extension exercise to the leg press exercise.
- Relax your hands, neck and face muscles during this exercise.

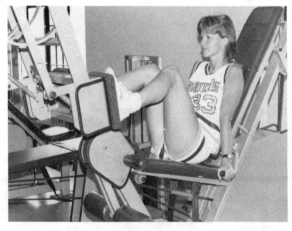

starting position

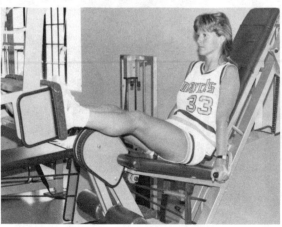

mid-range position

Nautilus Exercises: Leg Curl

Muscles used: Hamstrings

Starting position: Lie face down on the machine. Place the backs of your ankles under the roller pads with your kneecaps just off the end of the bench. Grip the handles loosely.

Description: Curl your legs upward, attempting to touch your buttocks with the roller pads. Pause and slowly recover to the starting position.

Points to emphasize:
- Your feet should be flexed with your toes pointing toward your knees throughout the exercise.
- Allow your hips to rise off the bench when nearing full contraction.

starting position

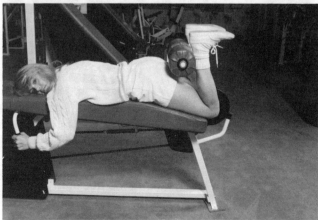

mid-range position

Nautilus Exercises: Hip Abduction

Muscles used: Gluteus medius, gluteus minimus

Starting position: Adjust the level on the right side of the machine until both movement arms are together; move the thigh pads to the outer position. Sit in the machine and place your knees and ankles on the movement arms. Your outer thighs and knees should be firmly against the resistance pads. Keep your head and shoulders relaxed against the seat back.

Description: Spread your knees and thighs to the widest possible position and pause, then return slowly to the starting position and repeat.

starting position   *mid-range position*

Nautilus Exercises: Hip Adduction

Muscles used: Adductor magnus

Starting position: Adjust the lever on the right side of the machine until the movement arms are as wide as comfortably possible. Move the thigh pads to the inside position. Sit in the machine and place your knees and ankles on the movement arms. Your inner thighs and knees should be firmly against the resistance pads. Keep your head and shoulders relaxed against the seat back.

Description: Press your knees and thighs smoothly together and pause, then return slowly to the starting position and repeat.

starting position

mid-range position

Nautilus Exercises: Heel Raise

Muscles used: Calves

Starting position: Adjust the belt comfortably around your hips. Stand and place the balls of your feet on the first step with your hands on the top step and your back perpendicular to the floor.

Description: Raise your heels as high as possible. Pause, then slowly recover to the starting position and repeat. Keep your knees locked throughout the exercise.

Points to emphasize:
- Do not lean forward.
- Attempt to flex your toes upward at the bottom of the movement to allow for maximum stretch.

starting position   *mid-range position*

Nautilus Exercises: Arm Cross

Muscles used: Pectoralis major, deltoids

Starting position: Adjust the seat until the center of each shoulder is directly beneath the center of the overhead cam. Fasten the seat belt. Place your forearms behind the movement arm pads. Grip the handles loosely (use whichever handle will place your elbows at ninety degree angles).

Description: Keep your head and shoulders back and push your elbows together until the movement arms touch. Pause, then slowly recover to the starting position and repeat.

Points to emphasize:
- Do not grip the handles too hard.
- Keep your head back and relaxed during the exercise.

starting position

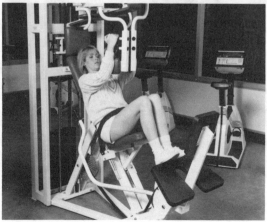

mid-range position

Nautilus Exercises: Rowing Torso

Muscles used: Posterior deltoids and rhomboids

Starting position: Sit with your back to the weight stack. Place your arms between the roller pads. Cross your arms, while keeping your elbows in the centers of the pads with your forearms parallel to the floor.

Description: Drive your elbows as far back as possible. Pause, then slowly return to the starting position and repeat.

Points to emphasize:
  • Do not lean forward.

starting position

mid-range position

Nautilus Exercises: Shoulder Shrug

Muscle used: Trapezius

Starting position: Take a seated position and place your forearms between the pads. Keep your palms open and facing upward. Straighten your back so that the weight stack is lifted. If the weight stack is not lifted in this position, place cushions on the seat for you to sit on.

Description: Raise your shoulders as high as possible. Pause, then slowly recover to the starting position and repeat.

Points to emphasize:
- Do not lean back or use your legs during the exercise.
- Do not straighten your arms.
- Check for good form and relaxed facial muscles in the attached mirror.

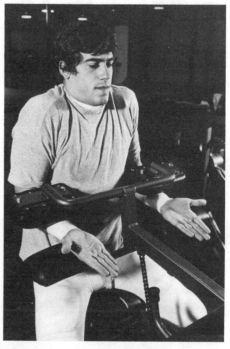

starting position   *mid-range position*

Nautilus Exercises: Chin-up*

Muscles used: Latissimus dorsi, biceps

Starting position: Place the crossbar in a forward position and adjust the carriage so that your chin is just over the bar when you are standing on the top step. Grasp the crossbar with an underhand grip and suspend your weight with your arms straight and your knees bent.

Description: Pull your body up until your chin is over the bar. Pause, then slowly recover to the starting position and repeat.

Points to emphasize:
- Negative-only repetitions can be performed, with or without a belt.
- When performing negative-only repetitions, begin in the up position and slowly lower your body, taking three to four seconds to descend, then climb the steps and repeat.

starting position

mid-range position

* To perform pull-ups, use an overhand grip instead of an underhand grip.

Nautilus Exercises: Pullover

Muscles used: Latissimus dorsi

Starting position: Adjust the seat so that the center of each shoulder joint is aligned with the center of the cam. Fasten the seat belt tightly. Depress the foot pedals to move the elbow pads forward. Place the backs of your elbows on the pads. Your hands should be open and leaning against the groove in the curved portion of the bar. Remove your feet from the foot pedals and allow your elbows to move back slowly to a stretched starting position.

Description: Rotate your elbows forward and downward until the crossbar touches your hips. Pause, then slowly recover to the starting position and repeat.

Points to emphasize:
- Your head and shoulders should remain against the back of the seat throughout the exercise.
- Keep your hands open and relaxed.
- Allow your elbows to stretch back as far as possible at the completion of each repetition.

starting position   *mid-range position*

Nautilus Exercises: Two-arm Curl

Muscles used: Biceps

Starting position: In a seated position, place your elbows on the pad and align them with the center of the cams. Adjust the seat so that your shoulders are lower than your elbows.

Description: Curl both of your arms until your wrists are just in front of your neck. Pause, then slowly recover to the starting position and repeat.

Points to emphasize:
- Keep your wrists in a locked position throughout the exercise.
- Do not allow your elbows to come off the pads during the exercise.
- Keep your head and torso in a vertical position.

starting position

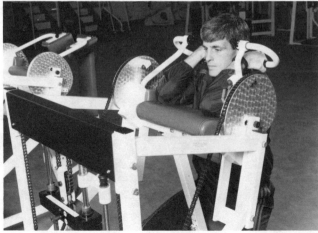

mid-range position

Nautilus Exercises: Tricep Extension

Muscles used: Triceps

Starting position: In a seated position, place your elbows on the pad and align them with the center of the cams. Place your hands inside the hand pads on each side of your neck.

Description: Extend both of your arms until your elbows are straight.

Points to emphasize:
- Keep your head and torso in a vertical position.
- Keep your elbows in constant contact with the pads.
- Pause for a moment in the mid-range position with your arms fully extended.

starting position

mid-range position

Nautilus Exercises: Wrist Curl

Muscles used: Forearm flexors

Starting position: Sit on the end of an exercise bench with your forearms resting on your knees. Grasp the handles with an underhand grip and raise them until the weight stack is lifted. Allow the handles to rest on your fingertips.

Description: Curl the bar up toward your elbows as far as possible. Pause, then slowly recover to the starting position and repeat.

Points to emphasize:
- Keep your forearms flat on your thighs throughout the exercise.
- Your wrists should be just over the ends of your knees.

starting position

mid-range position

Nautilus Exercises: Reverse Wrist Curl

Muscles used: Forearm extensors

Starting position: Sit on the end of an exercise bench with your forearms resting on your knees. Grasp the handles with an overhand grip and raise them until the weight stack is lifted. Allow the handles to rest on your fingertips.

Description: Curl the bar up toward your elbows as far as possible. Pause, then slowly recover to the starting position and repeat.

Points to emphasize:
- Keep your forearms flat on your thighs throughout the exercise.
- Your wrists should be just over the ends of your knees.

starting position

mid-range position

PARTNER RESISTANCE (PR) EXERCISES

Squat

Muscles used: All of the major muscles of the hips and legs

Starting position: To help you maintain balance, your partner stands on the opposite side of the leg that is being exercised. You should place an arm around your partner's shoulder for additional stability. Initially, most individuals do not possess enough strength to perform twelve reps. Therefore, your partner may have to help you recover to the starting position until you develop enough strength to do twelve reps correctly. Once you are strong enough to do this, your partner can begin to apply additional resistance to your hips.

Description: While squatting, you should attempt to keep your foot flat and your lower leg perpendicular to the ground. Lower your buttocks to a position behind your feet with the middle of your thigh parallel to the ground.

starting position

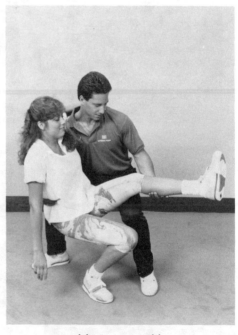

mid-range position

PR Exercises: Leg Press*

Muscles used: Gluteus maximus, quadriceps

Starting position: Lie on your back with one foot (or both feet) on your partner's chest. Use a pad between you and your partner to put your feet on during the exercise. Extend your arms for balance. The training partner's body weight serves as the resistance.

Description: Extend your leg (or both legs) slowly. Pause momentarily and then recover to the starting position. Do not lock out your knees in the mid-range position of the exercise.

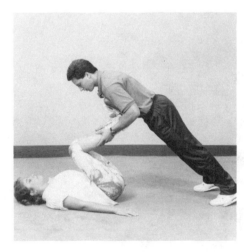

starting position

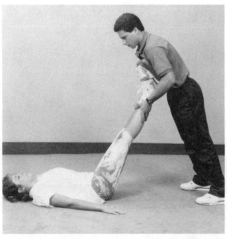

mid-range position

* This exercise can be performed with one leg at a time or using both legs simultaneously.

PR Exercises: Leg Curl

Muscles used: Hamstrings

Starting position: Lie face down. Your toes should be flexed to help increase the range of motion. The partner resistance is applied to the back of your heel or leg. If necessary, the partner uses both hands to spot.

Description: Raise your lower leg, flexing your toes toward your knee. Keep your foot in this position until your toes almost touch the ground during the lower phase. Raise your lower leg as high as possible and pause momentarily before recovering to the starting position.

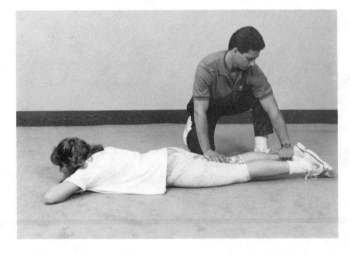

starting position

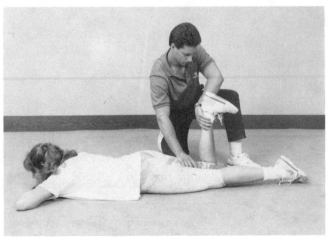

mid-range position

PR Exercises: Hip Flexion

Muscles used: Hip flexors

Starting position: Lie on your back. The partner resistance is applied just above your knee. Your partner must move backward and forward as you raise and lower your leg.

Description: To perform this exercise, flex your hip, raising your knee toward your chest, and pause momentarily in the contracted position before recovering to the starting position.

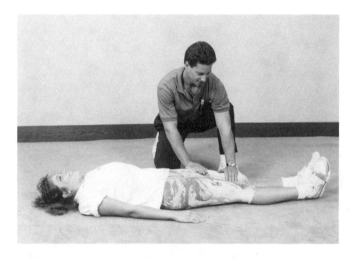

starting position

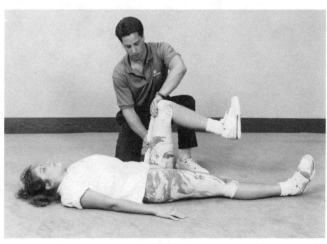

mid-range position

PR Exercises: Hip Abduction

Muscles used: Gluteus medius, gluteus minimus

Starting position: Lie on your side with your body extended and your legs slightly separated. Your upper and lower body should remain perfectly aligned throughout the execution of the exercise. Do not allow your upper body to bend forward at the waist. Your training partner applies resistance to the side of your leg. If you have a history of knee problems, the partner resistance should be applied just above your knee.

Description: During the execution phase, raise your leg sideward and upward as high as possible and pause momentarily in the contracted position before recovering to the starting position.

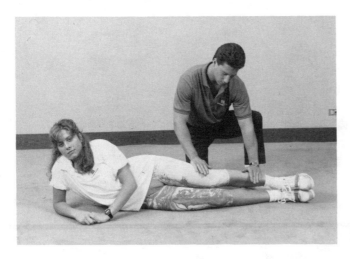

starting position

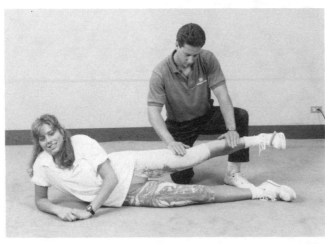

mid-range position

PR Exercises: Hip Adduction

Muscle used: Adductor magnus

Starting position: Lie on your back with your legs bent. The partner resistance is applied to the insides of your knees. Your partner must use caution as you approach the stretch position, because an injury could result if he applies too much resistance in the stretched position.

Description: To perform the exercise, raise your knees upward and toward each other to the contracted position. Pause momentarily and then return to the starting position.

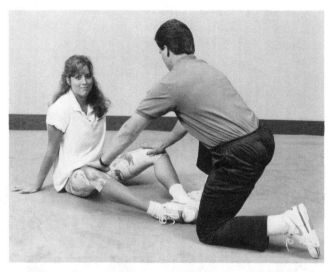

starting position

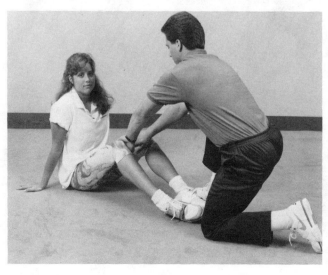

mid-range position

PR Exercises: Heel Raise

Muscles used: Calves

Starting position: Sit on the end of a table or exercise bench and hold onto the sides of the bench with your arms behind you. To obtain a stretch in the starting position, your toes must be elevated slightly. Your training partner provides resistance by sitting on a pad placed on your knees. If you prefer to perform the exercise from a standing position, your partner provides resistance by sitting on your lower back.   The exercise can also be performed one leg at a time (with or without a spotter).

Description: During the execution phase, elevate your heels as high as possible and pause momentarily before recovering to the starting position.

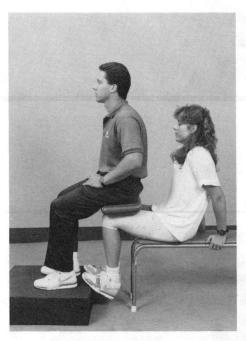

starting position

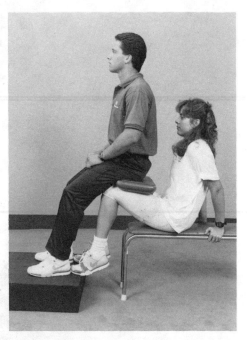

mid-range position

PR Exercises: Back Extension

Muscles used: Lower back muscles, sacrospinalis

Starting position: Secure your legs and hips to a table or exercise bench. Lower your upper body from the waist as far as it will go. The partner resistance is applied to your upper back by your partner.

Description: During the execution phase, raise your torso to a position parallel to the floor. Pause momentarily and then recover to the starting position. Extra caution should be used when performing this exercise, because most individuals ignore their lower back muscles. Also, the weight of your upper body alone may be more than enough resistance initially.

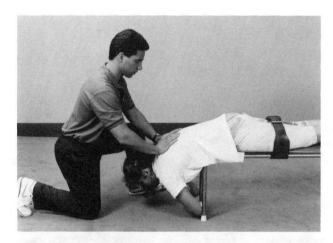

starting position

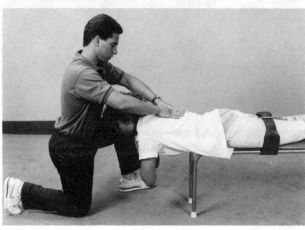

mid-range position

PR Exercises: Bent-arm Fly

Muscles used: Pectorals, anterior deltoid, subscapularis

Starting position: Lie on your back with your arms bent at ninety degrees with your upper arms perpendicular to your body.

Description: Raise your elbow(s) up and toward the midline of your body. Pause momentarily and then recover to the starting position. The partner resistance is applied to the inside of your arms. The exercise is easiest to spot one arm at a time, but it can be performed with both arms.

Points to emphasize:
- Because the muscles being exercised are stronger than the muscles used to spot, it is recommended that less time (two seconds) be allowed for the lowering phase if both of your arms are exercised simultaneously.

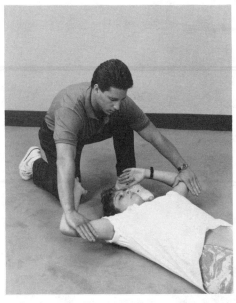

starting position

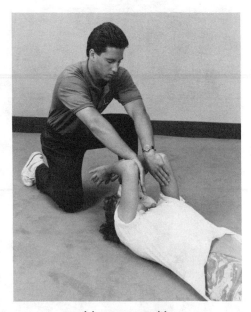

mid-range position

PR Exercises: Internal Rotation

Muscle used: Subscapularis

Starting position: Lie on your back on the floor with your arm bent down at a ninety degree angle and your upper arm perpendicular to your body. Your arm should be in a comfortable position. Do not hyperstretch your shoulder.

Description: Contract your rotators completely by moving your arm through a full range of motion around a vertical plane to your body. Pause before recovering to the starting position. The partner resistance is applied to your wrists throughout the exercise. Caution should be used to insure that you do not overexert. For some individuals a less than maximum effort is suggested for the first several workouts. Repeat the exercise with your other arm.

Points to emphasize:
- The range of motion of the subscapularis muscle varies from individual to individual.

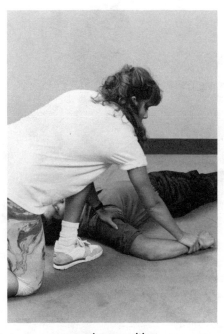

starting position

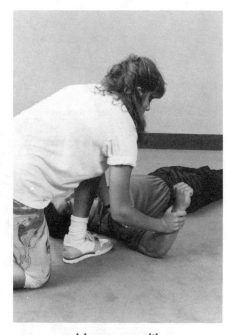

mid-range position

PR Exercises: External Rotation*

Muscles used: Rotator cuff muscles (infraspinatus and teres minor)

Starting position: The starting position is the same position assumed for the internal rotation exercise, except that your arm should be bent up.

Description: Move your arm toward your head through a full range of motion. Keep your upper arm in contact with the floor during the exercise. The partner resistance is applied to the back of your wrist. Caution must be used to be sure that you do not overexert. For some individuals, a less than maximum effort is suggested during their first several workouts. Repeat the exercise with your other arm.

Points to emphasize:
- The range of motion of the rotator cuff muscles varies from individual to individual.

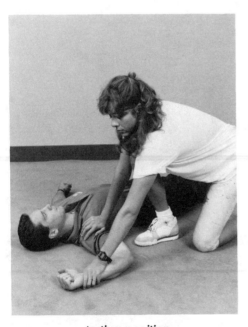
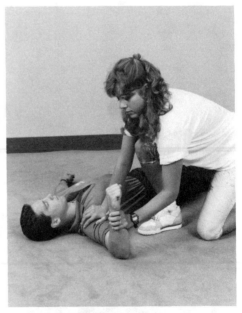

starting position   *mid-range position*

---

*   This exercise should not be used until you have mastered the pulling technique of the power high pull (free weight exercises).

PR Exercises: Shoulder Shrug

Muscles used: Trapezius

Starting position: Stand with your arms extended, holding a stick. An over and under grip should be used. If a stick is unavailable, your hands can be interlocked. The resistance is applied by the body weight of your training partner.

Description: Keeping your arms straight, shrug your shoulders as high as possible. Pause before slowly recovering to the starting position.

Points to emphasize:
* If your partner is too heavy she should bend her legs to make it easier for you.

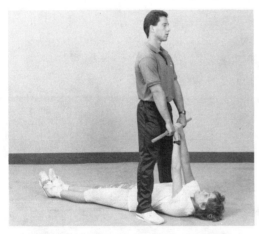

starting position

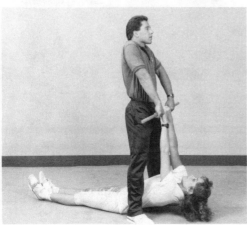

mid-range position

PR Exercises: Front Raise

Muscles used: Anterior deltoid, pectorals

Starting position: Assume a standing position and then stagger your feet
   approximately a half walking step apart for better balance. Your body
   should be erect and remain that way throughout the exercise. Extend
   your arms to the rear of your body with your palms facing backward.
   Your arms should be kept shoulder width apart throughout the execution.

Description: Raise your arms forward and upward to a position overhead
   and pause momentarily before recovering to the starting position. The
   partner resistance is applied to the backs of your wrists and hands
   throughout the execution of the exercise. To allow your arms to remain
   extended, your partner must move backward and forward as you raise
   and lower your arms.

starting position

mid-range position

PR Exercises: Bent-over Side Lateral Raise

Muscles used: Posterior deltoid, rhomboids, trapezius

Starting position: Your upper body should be bent at the waist and parallel to the ground with your arms extended and hanging down. Cross your arms to provide maximum stretching, and do not bend them.

Description: Raise your arms sideward and upward until they are parallel to the floor and perpendicular to your upper body. Pause momentarily in the contracted position and return to the starting position. The partner resistance can be applied to the back sides of your wrists or elbows.

Points to emphasize:
- Keep your head up and your back straight.
- Keep your back parallel to the floor.

starting position

mid-range position

PR Exercises: Back Pulldown / Bench Press

Muscles used: Rhomboids, pectorals, biceps, triceps, deltoids

Starting position: Lie on your back and thrust your arms overhead, shoulder width apart, palms up. Your partner should straddle your chest and face your arms and head. Your partner should place the bar (wooden dowel) in your hands.

Description: Pull the bar toward your chest against resistance provided by your partner. Pause, then push (press) the bar back to the starting position against your partner's resistance.

Points to emphasize:
- Both movements (the pulldown and the press) should be performed slowly, taking three to four seconds each.

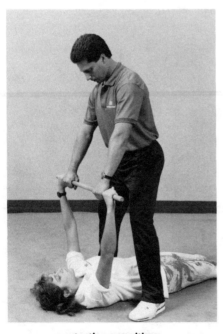

starting position

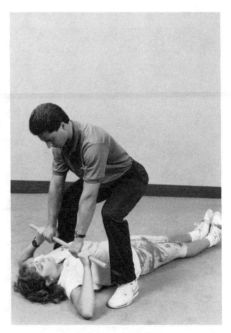

mid-range position

PR Exercises: Lat Pulldown / Seated Press

Muscles used: Latissimus dorsi, biceps, deltoids, triceps

Starting position: Assume a seated position with your legs crossed. Raise your arms overhead with your palms up. Your partner should stand behind you and place a knee in the middle of your back to give you stability, and he should place the bar (wooden dowel) in your hands.

Description: Pull the bar straight down and touch the base of the back of your neck. Your partner should provide resistance against your movement. Pause, then push (press) the bar back to the starting position against resistance provided by your partner.

Points to emphasize:
- Both movements (the pulldown and the press) should be performed slowly, taking three to four seconds each.

starting position

mid-range position

PR Exercises: Tricep Extension

Muscles used: Triceps

Starting position: Assume a seated position with your legs crossed. Lift your arms overhead, with your elbows pointed straight up, your hands behind your head and your palms up. Your upper arms should remain as close to your head as possible. Your partner should stand behind you with a knee in your back to give you stability. He should place the bar (wooden dowel) in your hands.

Description: Extend your arms overhead against moderate resistance provided by your partner. Once you reach a point where your arms are extended overhead, you and your partner reverse roles. Your partner forces the bar back down to the starting position against resistance provided by you. Note: The first phase of this exercise when you are doing the forcing is a concentric (positive) movement; the second phase when you are providing the resistance involves an eccentric (negative) movement.

Points to emphasize:
- Both movements (the concentric phase and the eccentric phase) should be performed slowly, taking three to four seconds each.

starting position

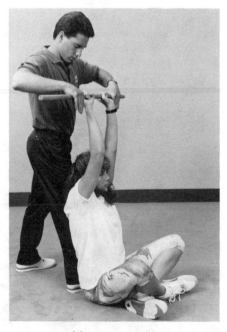

mid-range position

PR Exercises: Bicep Curl

Muscles used: Biceps

Starting position: Assume a standing position, with your feet approximately shoulder width apart and slightly staggered. Your hands should be at your sides with your palms facing forward. Your partner should stand facing you, and he should place the bar (wooden dowel) in your hands.

Description: Curl the bar up and toward your chest, working against moderate resistance provided by your partner. Once you reach the mid-range position of the exercise, you and your partner reverse roles. Your partner forces the bar back to the starting position against moderate resistance provided by you. The first phase of this exercise involves a concentric (positive) movement; the second phase involves an eccentric (negative) movement.

Points to emphasize:
 • Both movements (the concentric phase and the eccentric phase) should be performed slowly, taking three to four seconds each.

starting position

mid-range position

CHAPTER 4

PLYOMETRIC TRAINING

Plyometrics is a means of developing explosive power, which is a critical component of vertical jumping ability. Plyometrics is designed to enable athletes to combine strength and speed into power. Any activity in which a muscle is loaded eccentrically (lengthened) prior to contracting concentrically (shortened) is utilizing the plyometric principle. It is based on the concept that a muscle that is stretched prior to contraction will contract more forcefully. By loading a specific muscle eccentrically, you will, in effect, be stretching that muscle prior to contracting it. This action will result in a more forceful contraction.

The plyometric training concept was developed in the late 1960s by Russian track and field experts. The Russians concluded that since plyometric exercises are performed so explosively, they literally have a shock effect on the reactive ability of the neuromuscular system of the athlete. The net result is that the athlete's neuromuscular system adapts to the stresses imposed upon it by improving the ability of the muscle groups involved to respond quickly and powerfully to slight and rapid changes in the length of the muscles used in the movement. By using the stretch reflex (eccentric loading) as an integral part of his or her training, the athlete develops the ability to react more quickly.

Since time is a critical factor in your ability to apply force (POWER = FORCE X VELOCITY), improving your velocity will increase your power. In learning how to jump higher, it is important to develop leg power.

FUNDAMENTAL GUIDELINES AND TECHNIQUES

Like strength training programs, programs designed to make you jump higher that employ plyometric exercises must be governed by certain guidelines if you want to achieve maximum results. We recommend that you closely adhere to the following guidelines:

1. Emphasize the principles of demand (overload), progression and specificity when developing your program. As in a strength training program (refer to Chapter 3), there is no adequate substitute for intensity. Maximal intensity will yield maximal results. Perform each plyometric exercise as quickly as possible (i.e., load the muscle rapidly). As your body adapts to the stresses imposed upon it, gradually increase the load. Failure to do so may result in either a reduction in the gains achieved or in an injury, or both. Select exercises that will help you develop the muscles and specific skills for which your program is designed. The last two sections of this chapter present several examples of plyometric exercises that can be used to increase your vertical jumping ability and a sample program of plyometric exercises that can be incorporated into your overall training program.

2. Establish a strength base prior to starting plyometric training. When you are dealing with an activity like plyometric training that imposes great demands on not only the muscles but also the bone cartilage, tendons and ligaments involved in the movement, a properly developed strength base will reduce your chances of being injured. You should keep in mind at all times that plyometric exercises, because they are performed so explosively, place a tremendous amount of stress on your knee, hip and ankle joints.

3. Make warm-up and warm-down exercises an integral part of your plyometric training program. Because of the explosive nature of plyometrics, it is of the utmost importance that your body be properly prepared to undergo the stresses you are about to impose upon it. A warm-up period that includes stretching, calisthenics (some of which should, toward the end of your warming-up efforts, include quick, semi-explosive movements) and in-place running must precede your plyometric training. After you work out, you should perform similar warm-down exercises.

4. Perform each and every repetition of each and every plyometric exercise as precisely as possible using the proper mechanics. Learn

how each exercise should be performed and then take steps to insure that you perform it properly. Work out with a partner who is knowledgeable in the proper techniques for performing plyometrics and willing to provide you with the feedback necessary for you to achieve maximal results.

5. Perform undamped (without delay), versus damped (with delay), landings while doing plyometric exercises that involve jumping. A damped landing involves using extra movement in your foot or ankle joint when you land prior to jumping, (i.e., rolling your foot from head to toe or vice versa). An undamped landing requires that you maintain a locked ankle when you land on the ground, which will enable you to perform as quick a release as possible. The quicker you are able to switch from yielding work (the landing) to overcoming work (the jumping), the more powerful your response will be.

6. Include plyometric training in your overall developmental program for increasing your vertical jumping ability two to three days per week. Most athletes perform plyometric exercises before their strength training workout. While we recommend that plyometrics be done on the same days that you lift weights, it is not mandatory that you do so. However, it is important that, if you do both plyometrics and strength training on the same day, you perform plyometrics before you lift weights.

PLYOMETRIC DRILLS

Double Leg Bound

Muscles used: Major muscles of the legs and hips. The arm and shoulder muscles are also indirectly involved.

Starting position: Assume a half squat and hold your head up. Your arms should be held down at your sides, and your body should lean forward.

Description: Jump forward and upward as far as possible. Force should be provided by extending your legs and hips and thrusting your arms. During the jump, you should attempt to reach as high and as far as possible by fully straightening your body. Upon landing, recover to the starting position and immediately bound again.

Points to emphasize:

- Perform three sets of ten repetitions (double leg bounds) with about two minutes of rest between each set.

Plyometric Drills: Alternate Leg Bound

Muscles used: Flexors and extensors of the legs and hips

Starting position: Assume a comfortable standing stance, with one foot ahead of the other. Your arms should hang relaxed at your sides.

Description: Push off with your right leg and drive the knee of your left leg up toward your chest. Gain as much height and distance as possible before landing on your left leg. To gain forward momentum, swing both your arms forward as you bound. Upon landing, repeat the movement by pushing off with your left leg. Continue, alternating legs.

Points to emphasize:
- Perform either three sets of ten repetitions (per each leg) or perform three sets of forty yards each of alternate leg bounds.
- A variation of this exercise can be performed by preceding the bounding with a ten- to fifteen-yard sprint.

Plyometric Drills: Double Leg Box Bound

Muscles used: Major muscles of the legs and hips, the stabilizer muscles of the lower back and trunk areas and the shoulder muscles (indirectly)

Starting position: Assume a half-squat position with your feet placed slightly more than shoulder width apart, approximately two steps in front of the first box.

Description: Explosively jump up onto the first box. Upon landing, immediately jump up and out as far as possible and land on the ground, recovering to the starting position. Repeat this sequence as often as is required for the number of boxes you are using until all the boxes have been used. Once through all the boxes is considered a single set.

Points to emphasize:
- Perform three to five sets of the exercise with at least two boxes per set.
- Rest approximately two minutes between sets.

Plyometric Drills: Double Leg Speed Hop

Muscles used: Muscles of the legs and hips, specifically the gluteals, hamstrings, quadriceps, and gastrocnemius

Starting position: Assume a slight forward leaning stance, with your knees bent and your head up. Your arms should be at your sides.

Description: Jump as high as possible. Bring your knees high and forward with each repetition. Upon landing each time, immediately jump again using the same leg action. Your jump can be enhanced by flexing your legs completely before each jump so that your feet are under your buttocks and by swinging your arms upward during the jump to achieve additional thrust.

Points to emphasize:

- Perform three to five sets of ten repetitions. Rest one minute between each set.
- Keep in mind that your goal on each jump is to jump as high and as far as possible.

Plyometric Drills: Squat Jump

Muscles used: Hip flexors, quadriceps, gastrocnemius, hamstrings, and gluteals

Starting position: Assume a half-squat position, with your fingers interlocked behind your head. Your feet should be shoulder-width apart.

Description: Explode upward as high as possible. Upon landing, initiate another jump just prior to recovering the starting position (the half-squat position). Continue to repeat the sequence until the desired number of repetitions are performed.

Points to emphasize:
- Perform two to four sets of twenty repetitions.
- Rest one minute between each set.
- Strive to achieve a maximum height during each step.

Plyometric Drills: Box Jump

Muscles used: Major muscles of the legs, hips and lower back

Starting position: Assume a standing position with a slight forward lean. Your knees should be bent and your arms down at your sides.

Description: Jump explosively onto the box, using your arms to aid your thrust. Land on the box with both feet together. Upon landing, immediately jump back to the starting position. Repeat the sequence with a minimum amount of rest between repetitions until the desired number of repetitions for each set is performed.

Points to emphasize:
- Perform three to five sets of ten jumps.
- Rest one minute between each set.
- You can vary the exercise by alternating the directions that you jump. For example, you could jump off to the other side of the box.
- Concentrate on jumping each time as quickly as possible.
- Minimize the amount of time that your feet are in contact with either the ground or the box.

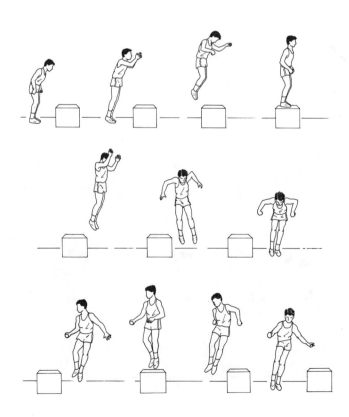

Plyometric Drills: Depth Jump

Muscles used: Quadriceps, hip girdle muscles, lower back muscles, hamstrings

Starting position: Stand at the edge of a box (or other elevated device, approximately twenty-four to thirty-two inches high), with the front of your feet slightly over the edge of the box. Your knees should be slightly bent and your arms held relaxed at your sides.

Description: Drop from the box (do not jump) to the ground. Land with your feet together and your knees bent to absorb the shock of the landing. Immediately upon landing, jump as high and as far as possible. Your jump should be initiated by swinging your arms upward and extending your body as high and as far out as possible.

Points to emphasize:
- Do three sets of ten repetitions.
- Rest one minute between each jump.
- A variation of this exercise is to execute another jump after the initial one.
- Strive to achieve maximum height and distance on each jump.

Plyometric Drills: Single Leg Stride Jump

Muscles used: Lower back, quadriceps, gluteals, hamstrings and hip flexors

Starting position: Stand next to and at the end of a bench or other elevated surface (e.g., bleachers). Your inside foot should be on top of the bench, and your arms should hang at your sides.

Description: Swing your arms upward and jump as high as possible by using the foot on the bench to exert power. Each time your outside foot touches the ground, repeat the action, using your inside foot to generate the force necessary to jump. Each jump will take you further down the bench. When you reach the end of the bench, turn around and reverse the positions of your legs. Repeat the movements in the other direction. Up and back once each way constitutes a single repetition.

Points to emphasize:
- Perform two to three sets of ten repetitions.
- Rest one minute between sets.
- Strive to achieve full height and body extension with each jump.

Plyometric Drills: Quick Leap

Muscles used: Hip flexors, quadriceps, hamstrings, gluteals, lower back and shoulder girdle muscles

Starting position: Stand facing a box about fifteen to twenty inches away. Your body should have a slight forward lean, with your knees bent slightly and your arms hanging at your sides.

Description: Explosively jump onto the box, swinging your arms energetically to gain additional thrust. During the jump, while in the air, try to keep your knees high and in front of your hips. Land flat-footed on the box in a semi-squat position to help absorb the shock. Upon landing, immediately jump explosively up and out as far as possible. During the jump, attempt to extend and straighten your entire body. Land flat-footed on the ground with your bent legs acting as a cushion against the shock of landing.

Points to emphasize:
- Perform three sets of ten repetitions of the exercise.
- Rest one minute between each set.
- This exercise can be varied by landing on the box with only one foot, and then performing the leap using only one leg.

Plyometric Drills: Depth Jump Leap

Muscles used: Quadriceps, gluteals, hamstrings, gastrocnemius and hip flexors

Starting position: Two boxes (one approximately fifteen to eighteen inches high and the other about twenty-four to thirty inches high) are required to perform this drill. The boxes should be placed approximately two feet apart. Stand on the higher box with your feet slightly off of the edge of the box (similar to the starting position for the depth jump drill). Your arms should be hanging at your sides, and your feet should be together.

Description: Drop off the higher box, as in the depth jump. Land on the ground with your feet together. Immediately jump explosively onto the lower box, and again land on both feet. As your feet come into contact with the lower box, leap upward and forward as far as possible. Use your arms and a full extension of your body to achieve maximum thrust. Finish by landing on both feet. Bend your knees to cushion the impact.

Points to emphasize:
- Perform three to five sets of ten repetitions.
- Rest one minute between each set.
- Concentrate on achieving an explosive depth jump, immediately followed by a maximum leap.
- A variation of the exercise can be performed by using one leg instead of two legs on the depth jump and subsequent leap.

CHAPTER 5

MENTAL TRAINING

The question of which attributes affect athletic performance has received a substantial amount of attention in sports literature. Accordingly, the perceived impact of genetic, physiological and biomechanical capabilities on athletic performance has been examined in considerable depth by numerous sport scientists. In recent years an additional factor has been accorded widespread recognition as a major determinant of athletic performance: the mental side of sport.

Individuals in the athletic arena—coaches and athletes alike—have come to recognize that the mental aspects of performance cannot be separated from the physical factors. As a result, mental training has assumed a critical role in many of the developmental efforts to improve athletic performance. These individuals are integrating many of the principles of effective psychological (mental) preparation in their training programs, just as they have employed exercise physiology and sports medicine principles over the years to enhance athletic performance.

For the athlete who would like to be able to jump higher, this chapter is an excellent companion to the previous chapters on strength training and plyometric training. From a rather extensive list of mental skills that have direct application on your potential for improving your vertical jumping ability, seven of these mental skills have been selected for discussion. An overview of each skill is presented, and a brief proposal on how to develop that specific skill is suggested.

Seven Mental Skills for Improving Your Vertical Jump

Skill #1: Relaxation

When a muscle is tense, it is contracting (shortening). This act of contraction involves your nerves as well. About half of the nerves in your body are involved in alerting your muscles with selected impulses. The problem occurs when your muscles receive too high a level of innervation. When this happens, the resultant high level of nervous tension actually causes your muscles to become rigid. In other words, excessive nervous tension is often accompanied by excessive *muscular* tension. As an athlete or coach, you have a critical need to be able to control the amount of muscular tension you experience, because too much muscular tension can interfere with the execution or performance of muscular skills. Vertical jumping is no exception.

The relevant question facing individuals who have too much tension is how to reduce this tension to a manageable level. Several different approaches and techniques have been identified for accomplishing this goal. Some of these methods will work better for you than others. The literature suggests that one of the most effective means of reducing tension is to regularly practice and use relaxation techniques.

Relaxation techniques generally can be categorized into either of two groupings: those that are considered "muscle-to-mind" (the somatic aspects) and those that involve "mind-to-muscle" (the cognitive aspects). Muscle-to-mind relaxation techniques require that you become sufficiently sensitive to tension so that you are able to recognize any level of tension in any given muscle. After you've mastered that capability, you then undergo training that will enable you to release the tension without being conscious of doing so. Basically, this group of relaxation techniques involves focusing on training one muscle at a time. You become sensitive to the level of tension in the muscle, let the tension go and then try to maintain the feeling of not having tension in that muscle without letting the tension return. Usually, you progress from one muscle group to another while engaged in this form of afferent nerve control training.*

Mind-to-muscle relaxation techniques, on the other hand, focus on controlling the stimulation of the central nervous system to a specific muscle.

_____

* A comprehensive explanation of several examples of muscle-to-mind relaxation techniques is presented in Dorothy V. Harris's book, THE ATHLETE'S GUIDE TO SPORTS PSYCHOLOGY.

Successfully employed, this form of nerve control will lead to a relaxation of the muscles. Examples of such efferent nerve control include meditation, autogenic training and imagery. Imagery will be discussed in greater detail in the section on skill #3.

Skill #2: Stress Management

Most athletes experience some degree of anxiety before participating in their athletic event. On one hand, a certain amount of anxiety is generally considered desirable, in that it reflects the readiness and general level of arousal the athlete has generated in anticipation of the event. Too much anxiety, however, can destroy an athlete's ability to concentrate and prepare for the competition. In turn, too much anxiety will have a pronounced negative effect on the performance of an athlete.

One of the most effective techniques for maximizing your athletic performance (in this case, your vertical jumping ability) is to learn how best to control the level of stress you encounter. Defined in this instance as the collective sum of any interruption or distraction that may interfere with your performance, stress can be managed to a certain degree. First, you must identify your optimal level of stress for peak performance. Once you've done that, you need to employ specific mental and physical techniques to help you reach and maintain that level. Each person has his or her own way of reacting to stress. What signs of stress do you feel or exhibit — negative thoughts, tense muscles, a dry throat, a decreased level of self-confidence? How do you react to these signs? Among the numerous possible steps for controlling stress, the literature suggests that two of the most effective techniques are to refocus your mind and attention internally and to employ specific relaxation techniques, such as controlled breathing. The main thing to remember is to identify what works for you and then use it.

Skill #3: Imagery

Imagery is probably the most widely applied mental skill used in athletics. Visualization, mental rehearsal, mental practice, kinesthetic experiencing and imagination are a few of the most commonly accepted terms for describing this skill. Although specific differences exist between each of these operational definitions, these differences are immaterial for most athletes. We suggest that for your purposes imagery basically involves recalling stored pieces of information from your memory bank and systematically rehearsing some specific behavior, such as vertical jumping.

Applying imagery to athletics is simple. For example, develop a clear mental picture of yourself perfoming an optimal vertical jump, and then imagine how that feels. Mentally practice performing the skill (e.g., vertical jumping) *exactly* the way that it should be performed. Learn what visual, auditory and kinesthetic cues will allow you to best develop a clear mental picture of specific athletic skill. Learn how to recognize your own cues and how to adopt those that are most effective for you. Remember that imagery is a learned skill that requires a great deal of effort, concentration and practice to master. When combined with physical practice, imagery can enhance parformance. It does not, however, involve either daydreaming or wishful thinking about unrealistic perceptions of athletic greatness.

Skill #4: Goal Setting

Your performance on a specific athletic or motor skill, like vertical jumping, at any given time is basically a function of your developed capabilities and your ability to execute those capabilities at an appropriate level in a specific situation. One of the primary factors that affects the degree to which you can maximize your performance is your level of motivation. Accordingly, it is not surprising that coaches traditionally have sought ways to motivate their athletes. In recent years, numerous sport scientists have concluded that the key to understanding and achieving a proper level of motivation in sports is goal setting.

Essentially, goal setting is identifying what you are trying to do or accomplish—jump higher, for example. Obviously, goal setting is integrally related to motivation. Your level of motivation affects the direction in which the goal is set, the effort you are willing to expend to achieve the goal and your persistence in attempting to accomplish the goal. In turn, proper setting of goals and regular evaluation of your progress toward achieving your goal has been shown to enhance performance and facilitate subsequent improvement. Goal setting gives you direction for your efforts. It can provide structure for your behavior both during training and competition. In most instances, goal setting will increase the likelihood of your using relevant strategies to achieve goals.

To maximize the benefits of goal setting, there are certain factors that you should consider when developing goals. In *The Athlete's Guide to Sports Psychology,** author Dorothy Harris recommends ten specific guidelines that should be followed when establishing goals:

- Put your goals in writing.
- Goals must be challenging but attainable, measurable, realistic and manageable.
- When two or three goals are established, they must be compatible.
- Goals should be flexible enough to allow for revision and change.
- Goals should have structured time frames or target dates.
- Priorities should be established for goals.

* Leisure Press, 1984.

- All factors relating to goal attainment should be taken into account.
- Goals should be stated to allow for evaluation of effort as well as performance.
- Goals should be related to the overall aim of performance.

Skill #5: Commitment

Equally important as establishing goals and priorities is making a commitment to pursue and attain those goals. Only you can determine the intensity of your commitment to achieving your goals. That commitment will, in turn, determine how much time and energy you are willing to expend to achieve a specific goal. When improving your vertical jump, progress is often measured in fractions of an inch. In a case such as this, it is important that you receive some degree of positive feedback regarding the reasons for your commitment and your expenditure of so much time and energy. Receiving such positive feedback and reinforcement on a regular basis will help sustain the sensory dimensions of sport—excitement, enthusiasm, challenge—that make your involvement in the event fun. If your participation is not satisfying, the likelihood of you continuing to spend the time and energy necessary for success is greatly reduced. Accordingly, we recommend that you continuously reevaluate your commitment and your reasons for pursuing your goals.

Skill #6: Concentration

Concentration involves the ability to attend to what is going on, the degree to which you can attend to what is going on, and the length of time you can continue to attend to what is occurring around you. Also referred to as selective attention, concentration is a skill that can be learned. It must be practiced regularly to be maintained at a high level of efficiency. The ability to attend to specific occurrences and ignore others while on the athletic field is obviously a desirable skill. The athlete who possesses the ability to put his or her mind on one thing at a time or on all the factors that relate to what is happening at a specific time will be a better performer, all things considered, than one who cannot. Simply stated, if you are unable to focus one hundred percent on what you are doing, then your performance cannot achieve its maximum level.

As an athlete, you need to learn where and when to focus your attention. You need to understand how attentional focus can improve your athletic performance. You need to develop the ability to control both the intensity and the duration of your concentrative skills as is appropriate to your personality and individual needs. You need to focus on minimizing—and hopefully eliminating—mental errors during your training and competitive bouts. Finally, in order to improve your concentration skills, you need to include basic concentration exercises (e.g., yantas, grid exercise, focusing on one thing) in your regular training regimen. Anxiety is dysfunctional to performance. If you can focus your attention on what you are about to do, it will be impossible to worry at the same time. In a single-minded fashion, focus on jumping higher. Your God-given abilities will do the rest.

Skill #7: Positive Thought Control

The inner dialogue of a champion athlete differs considerably from that of a loser before, during and after competition. Your inner thoughts reflect different feelings and perceptions. These feelings and perceptions, in turn, frequently have a way of becoming a self-fulfilling prohecy. As a result, in order to maximize your athletic performance, you need to learn how to control and direct your thoughts in a positive manner that will preclude undesirable emotional responses.

Your first step is to generate positive thoughts as much as possible. Among the numerous actions that will help you attain this goal are the following:

- Think positively. Remember that it is not the situation (the competition or the playing) that makes you nervous. You cause your own worry.

- Be realistic and objective in your thinking. To assume that things must be a certain way is to deal in fantasy. Be ready to deal with things as they are, not as you think they should be.

- You feel the way you think. Therefore, you have to change the way you think if you want to change the way you feel.

- We are all subject to failure. You must, within the framework of effective goal setting procedures, be able to adjust to failure.

Your second step is to control negative thoughts. As much as we would like everything to proceed and evolve in a predetermined pattern, sometimes it is impossible to avoid negative thoughts. As an athlete, you need to devise effective ways to cope with such thoughts. Among the steps that you could adopt are:

- Examine your negative thoughts to see if you could use them in a positive way to work out a solution.

- Identify the source of your negative thoughts and take corrective action to remove their origin (Note: many sport psychologists recommend that you keep a written record of your thoughts before, during and after both training and competition).

- Replace your negative thoughts with positive plans for the future.

- Substitute a neutral thought for a negative thought.

- Ignore your negative thoughts, which are otherwise unresponsive to solutions acceptable to you.

APPENDIX A

THE BACKMATE® WORKOUT PROGRAM

Of all the muscles involved in vertical jumping, among the largest and most important are the buttocks and the erector spinal (lower back) muscles. Although the squat exercise and the leg press exercise have traditionally been used to strengthen the buttocks, it is only the recent availability of the BackMate® apparatus* that has enabled coaches and athletes to effectively develop the erector spinal muscle groups through a full range of motion. In over five years of empirical efforts involving prototypes of this apparatus, every high school program that followed the BackMate® workout achieved substantial improvement in vertical jumping ability. Coaches involved with the program have been particularl y pleased with the fact that the BackMate® offers a highly efficient (less than two minutes per day per athlete), extraordinarily safe means of strengthening the lower back—an area of the body often ignored in many strength training programs.

Using the BackMate® apparatus, as Figures A.1 through A.5 illustrate, is a relatively simple task. 1) While you keep your knees locked, your partner raises your legs to the starting position (Figures A.1, A.2). In the first phase of the exercise, your lower back and hamstring muscles are stretched for thirty to sixty seconds (Figure A.3). 2) The second phase of the exercise involves strengthening your lower back and buttocks muscles. In this part of the exercise, you are required to perform a movement that involves forcing your legs downward—again while keeping your knees locked—against pressure exerted by your partner against your movement (Figure A.4). Your partner will permit you to move your legs slowly downward (taking approximately three to four seconds) to a position at approximately the height of your partner's knees. At that point your partner will command, *"Halt."* You then stop exerting a downward force, and your partner lifts your legs back to the starting position. This strengthening movement is repeated for a total

---

* The BackMate® apparatus evolved from the efforts of two West Point faculty members to indentify a safe, relatively inexpensive means of strengthening the lower back—not only to improve vertical jumping ability, but also to treat and prevent back pain. To date, a prototype of the BackMate® apparatus has been tested successfully as a means of dealing with back pain with over 200 cadets, USMA faculty members and members of the USMA community. As a device for increasing vertical jumping ability, it has been used successfully in more than 50 high schools across the United States. Additional information regarding BackMate® can be obtained by contacting the manufacturer: LIFEMATES / 9501 West Devon Avenue, Suite 203 / Rosemont, Illinois 60018.

of twelve repetitions.   3) The third and final phase of the BackMate® exercise involves performing the stretching phase (the aforementioned first phase) of the exercise again for an additional thirty seconds. After these exercises have been completed, bring your knees to your chest and pull on them firmly for ten to fifteen seconds (Figure A.5). The recommended protocol for using the BackMate® is one set of twelve repetitions, three to four workouts per week. If you lift weights, BackMate® exercises should be a regular part of your strength training program. Because BackMate® strengthens your lower back and buttocks muscles, these exercises should be performed as the first portion of your strength training program.

A.1 The subject lies flat on the BackMate® with the strap across her hips and her knees locked. Her partner lifts her legs to the starting position.

A.2 The starting position for the BackMate®.

A.3 Prior to performing the strengthening phase of the program, the partner stretches the subject for 30–60 seconds. The subject must keep her knees locked.

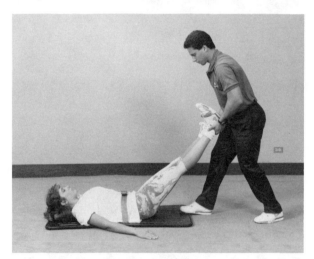

A.4 The mid-range position for the strengthening phase of the exercise. The subject forces her legs downward against moderate resistance provided by her partner. Once her legs reach an angle of 45° (to the knees of her partner), the repetition is completed. Her partner then raises her legs back to the starting position and another repetition is performed.

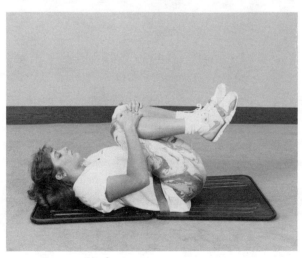

A.5 After the BackMate® exercises are performed, the subject brings her knees to her chest and firmly pulls on them for 10–15 seconds to further stretch the lower back.

APPENDIX B

THE ULTRA-ROPE® TRAINING SYSTEM

Rope jumping, in its basic form, can be viewed as a plyometric exercise. Specific muscles are loaded (from the point at which the rope is overhead and continuing on its downward path) and unloaded (from the point at which your body pushes off just before the rope passes beneath your feet). Similar to the plyometric exercises described in Chapter 4, rope jumping requires your body (primarily your leg muscles) to absorb energy and then turn that energy around (the lifting or propulsion phase), somewhat analogous to the action of a rubber band when it is stretched.

Rope jumping involves three phases. In phase one you bend your knees, "loading" your body for the jump. This movement is primarily eccentric. Phase two requires you to "push off" from the ground in a concentric action. It lasts until at least one foot touches the ground. This jumping movement is initiated as your ankles plantar flex and your knees and hips extend as the rope passes beneath your feet. The last part (phase three) of rope jumping is commonly referred to as the "landing" phase. It begins with one leg supporting your landing as you brace for the "shock absorption" of landing and extends to a point where both legs are supporting your body weight. At this point, your body re-establishes the conditions necessary for the loading phase (phase one) and is ready for another cycle.

WHY JUMP ROPE?

Many coaches and athletes have traditionally incorporated rope jumping into their conditioning programs for a variety of reasons—some more valid than others. The primary benefits of rope jumping are the development of specific motor skills, such as upper to lower body coordination, gross body equilibrium (balance), agility, kinesthetic awareness and limb speed. Provided your rope jumping routine is intense and of sufficient duration, you can also improve both your anaerobic and aerobic levels of fitness. In addition, depending on the individual, rope jumping may affect your level of muscular fitness—particularly upper body muscular endurance. Individuals who are active participants in sports involving the aforementioned motor skills (e.g., volleyball, basketball, football), are most likely to use rope jumping as a conditioning method.

A recent development in the area of rope jumping has been the weighted jump rope. Available in two-, three-, and four-pound sizes, the weighted jump rope is constructed of solid polyvinyl and comes with swivel handles that are designed to minimize strain on the exerciser's arms during the jumping workout. After several attempts by a variety of companies to manufacture a weighted jump rope, the rope that currently commands the lion's share of the ever-expanding market for such a device is called the Ultra-Rope®.*

The Ultra-Rope® is designed on the premise that the demands placed on you by having to accommodate the increased weight of the rope (as opposed to a regular rope) will elicit favorable changes in both selected components of fitness (aerobic fitness and muscular fitness) and selected motor skills and attributes (such as muscular power and vertical jumping ability). The nature of the demands involves dealing with the added momentum (mass times velocity) and force (mass times acceleration) that is produced during rope jumping while using the heavier rope. Although the precise effects of weighted rope jumping are still to be determined within well-controlled, scientific studies, the initial reports of several such rope users are highly favorable concerning the benefits of weighted rope jumping.

THE PROGRAM

A wide variety of possible routines exists for using the Ultra-Rope®. The recommended regimen, based on sound physiological training principles, suggests working out three times a week, in fifteen- to twenty-minute sessions. Each session consists of a series of continuous sets of a specified duration, interrupted only by thirty-second rest periods. Initially, each set should last for a minimum of thirty seconds and gradually increase in length as you become better able to perform (ideally, non-stop for the entire workout session). During each set, you should be able to jump at least sixty revolutions of the Ultra-Rope® per minute.

---

* According to the manufacturer, the Ultra-Rope® is currently being used in a number of successful intercollegiate athletic programs, including those at Duke University and the University of Kentucky. Additional information on the Ultra-Rope® can be obtained by writing to: Ultra-Rope / GARNEY INCORPORATED / 5460 33rd Street, S.E. / Grand Rapids, MI 49508 or by calling toll-free 1.800.23.ULTRA.

B.1

B.2

B.3

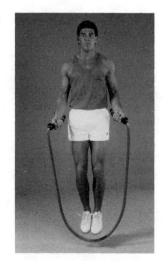

REFERENCES

Astrand, P.O. and K. Rodahl. *Textbook of Work Physiology: Physiological Basis of Exercise.* 2nd ed. New York: McGraw Hill, 1977.

Bedi, J.F., A. G. Gresswell T. J. Engel and S. M. Nicol. "Increase in Jumping Height Associated with Maximal Effort Vertical Depth Jumps." *Research Quarterly for Exercise and Sport,* 58:11–15, 1987.

Bosco, C. and P. V. Komi. "Mechanical Characteristics and Fiber Composition of Human Leg Extensor Muscles." *European Journal of Applied Physiology,* 41: 275–284, 1979.

Brooks, G. A. and T. D. Fahey. *Fundamentals of Human Performance.* New York: MacMillan Publishing Company, 1987.

Clarke, D. H. and F. M. Henry. "Neuromotor Specificity and Increased Speed from Strength Development." *Research Quarterly,* 32:315–325, 1961.

Clements, Lawrence E. "Power Relative to Strength of Leg and Thigh Muscles." *Research Quarterly,* 37:71–78, 1966.

Cratty, B. J. *Movement Behavior and Motor Learning.* Philadelphia: Lea and Febiger, 1973.

deVries, Herbert A. *Physiology of Exercise for Physical Education and Athletes.* 2nd ed. Dubuque, IA: Wm. C. Brown Company, 1974.

Edington, D. W. and V. R. Edgerton. *The Biology of Physical Activity.* Boston: Houghton Mifflin, 1976.

Gambetta, Vern. "Plyometric Training." *TAC's Track and Field Coaching Manual,* V. Gambetta, editor. Champaign, IL: Leisure Press, 1981.

Gennaro, A. R., A. H. Nora, J. J. Nora, R. W. Stander and L. Weiss. *Blakiston's Gould Medical Dictionary.* 4th ed. New York: McGraw Hill, 1986.

Guyton, Arthur, C. *Basic Human Physiology: Normal Function and Mechanisms of Disease.* 2nd ed. Philadelphia: W. B. Saunders Company, 1977.

Harris, D. V. and B. L. Harris. *The Athlete's Guide to Sports Psychology.* Champaign, IL: Leisure Press, 1984.

Hoeger, Warner W. *Lifetime Physical Fitness and Wellness.* Englewood, CO: Morton Publishing Company, 1986.

Korman, A. K. *The Psychology of Motivation.* Englewood Cliffs, NJ: Prentice Hall, 1974.

Lamb, D. R. *Physiology of Exercise: Responses and Adaptations.* New York: MacMillan Publishing Company, 1984.

Mathews, Donald K. *Measurement in Physical Education.* 5th ed. Philadelphia: W. B. Saunders Company, 1978.

Mountcastle, Vernon B. *Medical Physiology.* 14th ed. St. Louis, MO: C. V. Mosby Company, 1980.

Radcliffe, J. C. and R. C. Farentinos. *Plyometrics: Explosive Power Training.* Champaign, IL: Human Kinetics Publishers, In 1985.

Riley, Daniel P. *Maximum Muscular Fitness.* Champaign, IL: Leisure Press, 1982.

Riley, Daniel P., ed. *Strength Training by the Experts.* Champaign, IL: Leisure Press.

Roberts, G. C. and D. M. Landers, ed. *Psychology of Motor Behavior and Sport.* Champaign, IL: Human Kinetics Publishers, 1981.

Roy, S. and R. Irvin. *Sports Medicine: Prevention, Evaluation, Management and Rehabilitation.* Englewood Cliffs, NJ: Prentice-Hall, Inc., 1983.

Sage, George H. *Motor Learning and Control: A Neuropsychological Approach.* Dubuque, IA: W. C. Brown Publishers, 1984.

Schmidt, R. A., *Motor Control and Learning.* Champaign, IL: Human Kinetics Publishers, 1981.

Smith, Leon E. "Relationship Between Explosive Leg Strength and Performance in the Vertical Jump." *Research Quarterly, 32:405–408, 1961.*

Strauss, Richard H., ed. *Sports Medicine and Physiology.* Philadelphia: W. B. Saunders Company, 1979.

Suinn, Richard M. *Seven Steps to Peak Performance.* Toronto: Hans Huber Publishers, 1986.

Vander, A. J., J. H. Sherman and D. S. Luciano. *Human Physiology: The Mechanisms of Body Function.* New York: McGraw-Hill, 1975.

Warfel, John H. *The Extremities.* 4th ed. Philadelphia: Lea and Febiger, 1974.

Welford, A. T. *Skilled Performance: Perceptual and Motor Skills.* Glenview, IL: Scott, Foresman Co., 1976.

Wilken, Bruce M. "The Effect of Weight Training on Speed of Movement." *Research Quarterly.* 23:361–369, 1952.

Wilmore, J. H. *Training for Sport and Activity.* Boston: Allyn and Bacon, Inc., 1982.

Wilt, F. and T. Ecker. *International Track and Field Coaching Encyclopedia.* West Nyack, NY: Parker Publishers, 1970.

Young, J. Z. *Programs of the Brain.* New York: Oxford Press, 1978.

THE AUTHORS

Dr. James A. Peterson is a professor in the Department of Physical Education at the United States Military Academy. He received his B.S. degree in Business Administration from the University of California at Berkeley and did graduate work at the University of Illinois at Champaign, where he received his Ph.D in Physical Education in 1971. The author of nearly thirty books on sports and fitness, Dr. Peterson has appeared on several regional and national television shows, including ABC's *Nightline* and the *CBS Evening News.* Currently he resides in West Point, New York with his wife Susan.

Mary Beth Horodyski is a certified athletic trainer in the sports medicine section of the United States Military Academy's Department of Physical Education. She did her undergraduate work at Lock Haven University and received an M.S. in Physical Education from Iowa State University. She is a certified exercise test technologist and a certified fitness instructor from the American College of Sports Medicine. She resides in High Falls, New York with her husband Robert and their daughter Nicole Elizabeth.